Raising the Bar

Additional Readings in Psychology

Prepared by

Tony Romano

Bronwyn Bruton

National Textbook Company
a division of NTC/Contemporary Publishing Group
Lincolnwood, Illinois USA

ISBN: 0-538-42904-6

Published by National Textbook Company,
a division of NTC/Contemporary Publishing Group, Inc.,
4255 West Touhy Avenue,
Lincolnwood (Chicago), Illinois 60712-1975 U.S.A.

Manufactured in the United States of America.

00 01 02 03 04 05 06 07 08 09 VL 9 8 7 6 5 4 3 2 1

Contents

Chapter 1 The Field of Psychology

Who Is the Cat That Curiosity Killed?

Elizabeth Loftus

Elizabeth Loftus has been called the "diva of disclosure" because of her research into the subject of repressed memories. She is currently professor of psychology and adjunct professor of law at the University of Washington.

Speakers at university graduations give all kinds of advice. Where do they come up with it? Often they borrow from others and come up with something like "Always do right." This bit came from Mark Twain, who went on to explain that by following this advice you "will gratify some people and astonish the rest." Or, I once heard the advice, "Make yourself necessary to somebody." This came from Ralph Waldo Emerson. Now, I have nothing against such advice, coming as it has from two individuals who have made such lasting contributions to the world's culture. But is their advice practical? Is it memorable? Is it the one thing you'd like to say to new graduates, their families and friends?

Today, I'm going to leave you with one piece of advice, and, as a specialist in the area of memory, with a way of remembering that advice. You'll see that it's advice about a cat. Not just any cat, but a particular cat—the cat that curiosity killed. I'll come back to the curiosity cat, but first, how I got to that advice to begin with. . . .

I began my studies at the University of California in Los Angeles in the 1960s—a period of unrest and turbulence. When I started university, America had 80 million fewer people than it has today. I was also going to tell you that the music stores at that time had yet to stock a Beatles' album, but my advisors said that you wouldn't be very interested in that fact, and instead I should mention that it was before there were any Spice Girls CDs. I had no idea what I wanted to do in life. It was about the same time that one of our modern American heroes, John Glenn Jr., made being an astronaut seem like a good career. He had just orbited three times around the earth, travelling about 81,000 miles in five hours, before he splashed into the Atlantic Ocean. He was the first American to make such a flight. He made being an astronaut seem like fun—but there didn't seem to be any girl astronauts, so maybe that wasn't for me. I considered the possibility of becoming a mathematics teacher and briefly flirted with the idea of being a private detective or a stockbroker.

I spent a lot of time at university with my two best friends, Diana and Caron, going to these Friday night things called "Beer Busts." We spent way too much time drinking beer, flirting with the fraternity boys, and crying on each other's shoulders when one of them broke up with us. Things happened during those years that made me feel terrible, like the assassination of our president, John F. Kennedy.

And then I discovered psychology. It happened in an introductory psychology course, after which I gobbled up all the psychology that I could. Even after that I still wasn't quite sure what I would do with all that psychology. In fact, I left university into a world still full of unknowns, and headed north to graduate school. My brother David drove me those 400 miles to Stanford. When he dropped me off, I started sobbing—it was the first time that I would be living away from home and I was scared to death.

From *Skeptical Inquirer,* Nov–Dec 1998 v22 n6 p60(2). Used by permission of the *Skeptical Inquirer,* Box 703 Amherst, NY 14226.

At the same time, there was brewing excitement. . . . All I knew for sure what that I was going to study more psychology.

When I think back to those years, it is clear to me that one of the biggest impacts on my life revolved around my growing understanding of science—or, in my case (and the case of many of you here), psychological science. From my professors, and textbooks, and study groups with fellow students, I learned that science is not just a huge bowl of facts to remember. Science is a way of thinking. It's a process. In an article in a recent issue of the New Yorker that I read on the plane coming to England, one writer put it much more aptly: Science is based on a fundamental insight—that the degree to which an idea seems true has nothing to do with whether it is true, and the way to distinguish factual ideas from false ones is to test them by experiment.

Well, I learned rather well how to test ideas by experiment and applied that knowledge to one particular subject matter—human memory. Over the years I've conducted hundreds of experiments, and learned some pretty nifty things about the workings of the human mind. Discovering some fundamental facts about the malleability of memory has been a most exciting thing to do.

But the study of psychology also gave me a way of thinking about the ideas of other people. About twenty years ago, when the psychology books were telling us that memory is permanent, that once something is seen or heard and goes into memory, it stays there forever, I wondered "How do they know that? What's their evidence?" And I dug up the so-called evidence and investigated it as thoroughly as I could. I discovered it wasn't evidence at all.

You don't need to be a practicing psychological scientist to pick up some of these skills. Whether you go on to become a police officer or a private investigator, a therapist or a teacher, a playwright or a physicist, a geologist or a geographer, a software engineer or a statistician, it's possible to make use of one important gift that the study of the psychological science has given to many of us. That is the gift of knowing how to ask the right questions about any claim that someone might try to foist upon you.

The first important question, in my mind, is three or four words long: "What is the evidence?"

When someone tries to tell you that:

- Your astrological sign determines your personality . . . or
- Aliens are arriving in UFOs and abducting people, or
- Coffee is bad for you, or
- Satanic ritual abuse is rampant, or
- Tenure is bad for the university . . .

. . . It should be almost automatic to ask, "What's the evidence?" Now, let me emphasize that, in using these particular examples, I'm not trying to suggest that they are all examples of what the evolutionary biologist Richard Dawkins has called "pernicious rubbish on an almost astrological scale." I'm only suggesting that it should be almost automatic to ask about any idea, "What's the evidence?"

Now, as psychologists we don't stop there. We can get even more specific about what we ask next:

- What kind of study was done?
- What was the dependent variable?
- Was there a control group?
- What kinds of statistical tests were used to analyze the data?
- Has the study been replicated?

What we're really asking here is question Number Two: "What exactly is the evidence?"

Some evidence is so flimsy or fragile that it is not really evidence at all. For example, as I and others have shown, some kinds of eyewitness testimony is so fraught with the probability of error that it is not really evidence at all, and to consider it so can sometimes lead to grave miscarriages of justice.

So these questions about evidence are valuable to be asking over and over in life.

There is a wonderful cartoon that appeared recently in Parade magazine, a magazine that reaches some 80 million people in America.

And here's where we get to that cat. Picture this: Mother and little Son are sitting at the kitchen table. Apparently Mother has just chided Son for his excessive curiosity. The Son rises up and barks back:

"Curiosity killed what cat?
What was it curious about?
What color was it?
Did it have a name?
How old was it?"

I particularly like that last question. Maybe the cat was very old, and died of old age, and curiosity had nothing to do with it at all.

So in closing, I remind you that speakers at university graduations give advice freely:

Go forth.
Always do right.
Be true to yourself.
Make yourself necessary to somebody.
Wear sunscreen.

It's all good, but, my pick for the one advice morsel to suggest to you is simple. Remember to ask the questions that good psychological scientists have learned to ask: "What's the evidence?" and then "What exactly is the evidence?" And if you forget these questions, then just try asking for the name or the age of the cat that curiosity killed.

❦❦❦

Name ______________________ Date ______________ Period ________

Chapter 1

Who Is the Cat That Curiosity Killed?

1. According to the article, "the degree to which an idea seems true has nothing to do with whether it is true." Why is this important to the author's argument?

2. According to the author, can evidence be accepted uncritically?

3. What is the significance of the story of the curiosity cat?

Name ______________________ Date ______________ Period ________

Chapter 1

Who Is the Cat That Curiosity Killed?

4. Do you think that memory is a reliable form of evidence? Give your reasons.

5. Write a paragraph describing an experience or an intellectual discovery that made an impact on your life. In what way did that experience or discovery influence you?

Folk Wisdom: Was Your Grandmother Right?

Robert Epstein

Robert Epstein received his Ph.D. from Harvard University under the guidance of B. F. Skinner. His scholarly contributions and achievements have been primarily in the field of cognition, creativity, and behavior.

The table next to me at Fillipi's restaurant was a noisy one. Two men and two women in their 20s and 30s were arguing about a relationship issue. One of the men—call him Male #1—would soon be leaving the country for six months. Would the passion he shared with his beloved survive? The exchange went something like this:

Female #1 (probably the girlfriend): "When you really love someone, being apart makes you care even more. If someone is good to you, you sometimes take that for granted when the person is around every day. But when he's gone, all that good treatment is gone, too, and you realize just how much you had. You really start to yearn for him."

Male #2 (looking lustfully at Female #1, even though he seemed to be with the other woman): "That's right. The same thing happens when your parents die. You really start to miss and appreciate them. You even rewrite the past, forgetting the bad things and focusing on the good times and the kindness they showed you."

Female #1 (starting to look lovingly at Male #2): "Exactly. Everyone knows that absence makes the heart grow fonder."

Then Male #1, the one probably on his way to Thailand, spoke up. "Well, but . . ." He faltered, thinking hard about going on. All eyes were on him. He took a deep breath.

And then he said, slowly and deliberately, "But don't we also say, 'Out of sight, out of mind'?"

This was not good for anyone's digestion. Female #1's face turned the color of marinara sauce. Male #2 smiled mischievously, presumably imagining himself in bed with Female #1. Female #2 looked back and forth between her date and Female #1, also apparently imagining them in bed together. And Male #1, not wanting to face the carnage, lowered his eyes and tapped out a strange rhythm on the table top with his fork. Was he thinking about the classy Thai brothels he had read about on the Internet?

Truth or Poppycock?

"Absence makes the heart grow fonder" and "Out of sight, out of mind" are examples of folk wisdom—folk psychology, you might say. All cultures pass along wisdom of this sort—sometimes in the form of proverbs; sometimes through songs (remember Paul Simon's "Fifty Ways to Leave Your Lover"?), rhymes (Mother Goose), or stories (Aesop's fables); sometimes through laws and public information campaigns ("Stay alive, don't drink and drive"); and always through religion ("Do unto others as you would have them do unto you").

But folk wisdom is an unreliable, inconsistent kind of wisdom. For one thing, most proverbs coexist with their exact opposites, or at least with proverbs that give somewhat different advice. Does absence truly make the heart grow fonder, or are loved ones out of mind when they're out of sight? And isn't variety the spice of life? (If Male #1 had come up with *that* one, he might have been murdered on the spot.)

Do opposites attract, or do birds of a feather flock together? Should you love the one you're with, or would that be like changing horses in midstream? We all know that he who hesitates is lost, but doesn't haste make waste, and isn't patience a virtue, and don't fools rush in, and aren't you supposed to look before you leap?

And, sure, money is power, but aren't the best things in life supposed to be free? And since time is money, and money is power, and power corrupts, does that mean time also corrupts? Well, maybe so. After all, the Devil finds work for idle hands.

I've only covered a few well-known proverbs from the English-speaking world. Each culture passes along its own wisdom, which is not always meaningful to outsiders. In India, for example, people say, "Call on God, but row away from the docks," and Romanians advise, "Do not put your spoon into the pot that does not boil for you." In Bali they say, "Goodness shouts and evil whispers," while in Tibet the message is, "Goodness speaks in a whisper, but evil shouts."

You get the idea. Proverbs that relay wisdom about how we're supposed to live do not necessarily supply useful or reliable advice. In fact, proverbs are sometimes used merely to justify what we already do or believe, rather than as guidelines for action. What's more, we tend to *switch* proverbs to suit our current values and ideals. A young man might rationalize risky action by pointing out that "You only live once"; later in life—if he's still around—he'll probably tell you, "Better safe than sorry."

Is the situation hopeless? Can we glean any truths at all from the wisdom of the ages?

The behavioral sciences can help. Science is a set of methods for testing the validity of statements about the world—methods for getting as close to "truth" as we currently know how to get. Psychologists and other scientists have spent more than a century testing the validity of statements about human behavior, thinking, and emotions. How well does folk psychology stand up to scientific inquiry? What do we find when we test a statement like "Absence makes the heart grow fonder"? If, as I do, you sometimes rely on folk wisdom to guide your actions or teach your children, this is a question well worth considering.

Here's how five common proverbs measure up to behavioral research.

Confession Is Good For the Soul

Psychologists don't study the soul, of course. But, says psychologist James W. Pennebaker, Ph.D., "If we define 'soul' loosely as who you are, how you feel about yourself, and how healthy you are, then confession is good for the soul." Pennebaker, a researcher at the University of Texas at Austin, is one of several behavioral scientists who have looked carefully at the results of "self-disclosure"—talking or writing about private feelings and concerns. His research suggests that for about two-thirds of us, self-disclosure has enormous emotional and physical benefits. Pennebaker's newly revised book, *Opening Up: The Healing Power of Expressing Emotion,* summarizes 15 years of compelling research on this subject.

Self-disclosure, as you might expect, can greatly reduce shame or guilt. In fact, studies of suspected criminals showed that they acted far more relaxed after confessing their crimes—despite the fact that punishment now awaited them. Self disclosure may also provide the power behind talk therapy. "The fact that self-disclosure is beneficial," says Pennebaker, "may explain why all forms of psychotherapy seem to be helpful. Whether the therapy is behavioral or psychoanalytic, in the beginning the clients tell their stories."

Perhaps most intriguing are the physical effects of "confession." Pennebaker has found that self-disclosure may actually boost the immune system, spurring production of white blood cells that attack invading microorganisms, increasing production of antibodies, and heightening the body's response to vaccination.

But what about those other proverbs that advise us to keep our mouths shut? "Let sleeping dogs lie." "Least said is soonest mended." "Many have suffered by talking, few by silence." Can self-disclosure do harm? According to Pennebaker, self-disclosure is not likely to be beneficial when it's forced. University of Notre Dame psychologist Anita Kelly, Ph.D., has suggested, moreover, that revealing secrets may be harmful if the confidant is likely to be judgmental. And a 1989 study conducted by Maria Sauzier, M.D., of Harvard Medical School, showed that people often regret disclosures of child abuse. Sauzier found that nearly half of the parents whose children had disclosed sexual abuse (usually to the other parent or a therapist) felt that both the children and the families were harmed by the disclosures. And 19 percent of the adolescents who confessed that they had been abused regretted making the disclosures. In general, however, confession seems to be a surprisingly beneficial act.

All Work and No Play Makes Jack a Dull Boy

To me, the most frightening scene in the movie *The Shining* was the one in which actress Shelley Duvall, concerned that her husband (Jack Nicholson) was going crazy, approached the desk at which he had spent several months supposedly writing a novel. There she found hundreds of pages containing nothing but the sentence, "All work and no play makes Jack a dull boy" typed thousands of times on a manual typewriter. I've always wondered who did all that typing! And I've also wondered about the truth of the proverb. Once again, we're also faced with contradictory bits of folk wisdom that urge us to work until we drop: "Rest makes rusty." "Labor warms, sloth harms." "Labor is itself a pleasure."

Is too much work, without the balance of leisure activity ("play"), actually harmful? Research suggests that the answer is yes, with one possible exception: if you love your work—in other words, if you've been able to make your *avocation* and *vocation*—then work may provide you with some of the benefits of play.

In the 1940s, anthropologist Adam Curle pointed out that the distinction between work and leisure seems to be an unfortunate product of modern society. In many traditional cultures, he wrote, "there is not even a word for work." Work and play "are all of a piece," part of the integrated structure of daily living. But modern society has created the need for people to earn a living, an endeavor that can be difficult and can easily get out of hand. Hence, the modern pursuit of "leisure time" and "balance"—correctives for the desperate measures people take to pay their bills.

Study after study confirms the dangers of overwork. It may or may not make you a dull person, but it clearly dulls your mind. For example, recent research on fire fighters by Peter Knauth, Ph.D., shows that long work shifts increase reaction time and lower alertness. And studies with emergency room physicians show that overwork increases errors and impedes judgment. Indeed, a Hollywood cameraman, coming off an 18-hour work shift, made news recently when he lost control of his car and died in a crash.

Conversely, leisure activities have been shown in numerous studies by researchers Howard and Diane Tinsley, Virginia Lewis, and others, to relieve stress, improve mood, increase life satisfaction, and even boost the immune system.

Curiously, the hard-driven "type A" personalities among us are not necessarily Dull Jacks. According to a recent study of more than 300 college students by Robert A. Hicks, Ph.D., and his colleagues, type-A students claim to engage in considerably more leisure activities than their relaxed, type-B counterparts. Type As may simply live "more intensely" than type Bs, whether they're on the job or goofing off.

The distinction between work and play is, to some extent, arbitrary. But it's clear that if you spend too much time doing things you don't want to do, your performance, health, and sense of well-being will suffer.

Boys Will Be Boys

The widely held (though politically incorrect) belief that boys are predisposed from birth to feel, learn, and perform differently from girls is strongly supported by research. For example, boys are, on average, considerably more aggressive than girls. They are left-handed more frequently than girls and tend to be better at math and at spatial rotation tasks. Girls, meanwhile, may perform certain kinds of memory tasks better. They also start talking earlier than boys, and, at the playground, they're more likely to imitate boys than boys are to imitate girls. And boys tend to listen more with their right ear, while girls tend to listen with both ears equally. These findings generally hold up cross-culturally, which suggests that they are at least somewhat independent of environmental influences. Upbringing plays an important role in gender differences, of course—even in the first days after birth, parents treat boys babies differently from girls—but converging evidence from psychology, neuroscience, and evolutionary biology suggests that many gender differences are actually programmed from birth, if not from conception.

Since the brain is the mechanism that generates behavior, where we find behavioral differences, we should also find neurological differences. Indeed, recent research suggests a host of differences between male and female brains. For example, although, on average, male brains are larger than female brains, the hemispheres of the brain seem to be better connected in females, which may help explain why females are more sensitive and emotional than males.

Behavior is also driven by hormones. Here, too, there are significant gender differences. From birth, testosterone levels are higher in males, which helps to account for males' aggressiveness. June Reinisch, Ph.D., then at Indiana University, studied boys and girls whose mothers had been exposed to antimiscarriage drugs that mimic testosterone. Not surprisingly, she found that these children of both sexes were considerably more aggressive than their counterparts with normal testosterone levels. But even among the exposed children, the boys were more aggressive than the girls.

So boys will indeed be boys (and, by implication, girls will be girls). But this is only true "on average." Male and female traits overlap considerably, which means that a particular male could be more emotional than most females and a particular female could be better at math than most males. To be fair, you have to go case by case.

Early to Bed, and Early to Rise, Makes a Man Healthy, Wealthy, and Wise

This proverb, often attributed to Ben Franklin, actually seems to have originated in the late 1400s, and Franklin may have lifted it from a collection of adages published in 1656. Historical trivia aside, research on sleep suggests that the proverb gives sound advice—but only because our culture is out-of-synch with the biology of nearly half the population.

Here's how it works: it's long been known that the body has natural rhythms. Those that occur on a 24-hour cycle are called "circadian" and include cycles of temperature change, wakefulness, and eating. For most people, these cycles are highly resistant to change. This much you probably have heard, but what you might not know is that there are two distinctly different circadian rhythm patterns. "Larks—who show what researchers call "morningness" (honest!)—are people whose cycles peak early in the day. Not surprisingly, larks awaken early and start the day strong. "Owls"—people inclined toward "eveningness"—peak late in the day. In both cases, the peaks are associated with better performance on memory tasks, quicker reaction times, heightened alertness, and cheerful moods. Some people are extreme larks or owls, others are moderates, and a few fit neither category.

There's a problem here, especially if, like me, you're an extreme owl. The trouble is that many important human activities—business meetings, job interviews, weddings, classes, and so on—are conducted during daylight hours, when larks have a distinct advantage. Not surprisingly, owls spend much of their time griping about how out-of-synch they seem to be.

A 1978 study of college students by Wilse B. Webb, Ph.D., and Michael H. Bonnet, Ph.D., of the University of Florida, paints a grim picture for people like me: "Larks reported waking up when they expected to, waking up feeling more rested, and waking up more easily than the owls." Larks also reported having "fewer worries" and getting "more adequate sleep," and they awakened feeling physically better than owls. The differences were even greater, moreover, when owls tried to adapt to the lark sleep pattern. What's more, these problems can impair not only owls' sense of restedness but also their bank account; a study of Navy personnel suggests that people who sleep well make considerably more money than people who sleep poorly.

The long and short of it is that if your biorhythms allow you easily to "go to bed with the lamb and rise with the lark" (another old proverb), you may indeed end up with more money, better health, and more life satisfaction—but only because your internal clock is more in-synch with the stock exchange.

Spare the Rod and Spoil the Child

A recent headline in my local newspaper proclaimed, "Spanking Backfires, Latest Study Says." I cringe when I see stories like this, because I believe they ultimately harm many children. People have come to confuse discipline with "abuse," which is quite a different beast. "Discipline"—whether in the form of "time outs," reprimands, or spankings—is absolutely necessary for parenting. Extensive research by psychologist Diana Baumrind, Ph.D., and others, has shown that permissive parenting produces children who can't handle independence and are unable to behave in a socially responsible manner. A great many social problems that we face today may be the inadvertent product of a generation of well-meaning, misinformed, overly-permissive parents.

However, if all you provide is discipline, without affection and emotional support—the "authoritarian" parenting style—you can damage your children. Offspring of authoritarian parents tend to be hostile and defiant, and, like the victims of permissive parents, they too have trouble with independence.

The most effective parenting style involves both a high level of discipline and ample affection and support. That's the best approach for producing children who are self-reliant, socially responsible, and successful in their own relationships, research shows.

In the latest anti-spanking study, published in August by University of New Hampshire sociologist Murray Straus, Ph.D., children between the ages of 6 to 9 who were spanked more than three times a week displayed more misbehavior two years later. Doesn't this show that spanking causes misbehavior? Not at all. Correlational studies are difficult to interpret. Perhaps without those spankings, the kids would have been even worse off. It's also possible that many of these spankings were unnecessary or excessive, and that it was this inappropriate discipline that sparked the later misbehavior.

Conversely, at least eight studies with younger kids show that spanking can indeed improve behavior. The age of the child, in fact, is probably important. Children under the age of six seem to regard spanking as a parent's right. But older kids may view it as an act of aggression, and in such cases spanking's effects may not be so benign.

Punishment, verbal or physical, applied in moderation and with the right timing, is a powerful teaching tool. It should not be the first or the only tool that a parent uses, but it has its place.

Truth à La Carte

But what about the restaurant debate? Does absence make the heart grow fonder or not? Alas, not enough research has been conducted to shed much light on this question. We do know that "out of sight, out of mind" is true when we're fresh from the womb; young babies will behave as if a boy has vanished into thin air when the toy is moved out of sight. But our memories quickly improve. Research conducted by Julia Vormbrock, Ph.D., and others, shows that children grow more fond of their caregivers when they're separated from them—

at least for a few days. After two weeks of separation, however, most children become "detached," reports Vormbrock.

Psychologist Robert Pelligrini, Ph.D., once asked 720 young adults about separation, and two-thirds said that "absence makes the heart grow fonder" seemed more true than "out of sight, out of mind." A poll, however, doesn't tell us much about the truth of the matter. To settle things, we'll need an experiment. Hmmm. First we'll need 100 couples, whom we'll give various tests of "fondness." Then we'll assign, at random, half of the couples to a Control Group and half to an Absence Group. Next we'll separate the partners in each couple in our Absence Group by, say, 1,000 miles for six months—somehow providing jobs, housing, and social support for every person we relocate. Finally, we'll readminister our fondness tests to all 100 couples. If we find significantly greater levels of fondness in the separated couples than in the unseparated couples, we'll have strong support for the idea that absence makes the heart grow fonder.

Any volunteers? What? You would never subject yourself to such an absurd procedure? Well, fortunately, no one would ever conduct such research, either.

And that's the bottom line: the behavioral sciences can provide useful insights about how we should lead our lives, but there are limits to the kind of research that can be conducted with people. Folk wisdom may be flawed, but, in some instances, it's all we've got or will ever have. So don't put all your eggs in one basket.

❦❦❦

Name ______________________ Date ____________ Period ________

Chapter 2

Folk Wisdom: Was Your Grandmother Right?

1. How does the author define folk wisdom?

2. Why did Epstein look closely at five proverbs? What was he trying to determine?

3. What did one researcher discover about the validity of the proverb *confession is good for the soul?*

Name ____________________ Date ____________ Period ________

Chapter 2

Folk Wisdom: Was Your Grandmother Right?

4. What distinction does the author make between discipline and abuse when looking at the proverb *spare the rod and spoil the child?*

5. What is your opinion on whether absence makes the heart grow fonder or not? Give reasons to support your answer.

The Fiction of the Reasonable Man

Richard Restak, M.D.

Richard M. Restak is clinical professor of neurology, George Washington University School of Medicine and Health Sciences, Washington, D.C. He is the author of numerous books, including Receptors *(1994) and* The Modular Brain *(1994).*

The actions of Bernhard Goetz were not those of a reasonable person.

A lawyer said that to me at a dinner party at the time of the trial of Bernhard Goetz, the "subway vigilante" accused of shooting four teenagers he stated were about to attack him.

Another dinner guest added: "The jury is going to have to examine the circumstances under which every bullet was fired and ask themselves, 'Was this the behavior of a reasonable person?' If there's any indication that even one of those shots was unnecessary, Goetz should be found guilty."

What they were referring to was the ruling by New York State's Court of Appeals in July of 1986 that a claim of self-defense (such as Goetz had made against charges of attempted murder and assault) must be judged by the dual standard of "reasonableness." During the trial the jurors were asked to determine not only that Goetz subjectively believed that he was acting reasonably, but that on an objective level his actions were those any "reasonable man" would pursue in the same circumstances.

As a neurologist and neuropsychiatrist with over a decade of experience in conducting pretrial interviews of individuals who have acted violently, I believe the "reasonable person" argument an illogical and outdated approach to fully understanding events in the Goetz case and other selective instances of violence. On the basis of what I know about the human brain, I'm convinced that no one acts reasonably when feeling threatened by death or severe bodily harm.

Deep within every reasonable person's brain is the limbic system, an ancient interconnected network of structures that anatomically and chemically have changed little over hundreds of thousands of years. We share these structures with jungle animals, as well as animals that many reasonable people keep as pets. Under conditions of extreme duress the limbic system is capable of overwhelming the cerebral cortex, wherein many of the reasonable person's most reasonable attributes—like interpretation, judgment, and restraint—are formulated.

The limbic system (from the Latin *limbus,* meaning border or seam) lies along the margin of the cerebral cortex and includes the amygdala, hippocampus, and other components, which interact directly with the thalamus and hypothalamus below. Taken together, they govern aggressive behavior.

Malfunctions in the system or its various neurotransmitters (chemicals that relay signals among brain parts) can cause temporarily deranged behavior. Such behavior can be chemically induced with such compounds as PCP ("angel dust"), which acts on the hippocampus and induces impulsive behavior; or it can be suppressed with drugs such as lithium, which boosts the level of a neurotransmitter called serotonin, important in the reduction of aggression.

In most instances the limbic system is an asset. Without it, few of our ancestors would have survived to enable us to be here asserting our reasonableness.

Occasionally the limbic system can malfunction because of a pathological condition, such as a tumor, or for other reasons still unknown. It overwhelms rationality, resulting in panic attacks, outbursts of rage, perhaps even murder.

- An executive on his way to an important business meeting begins to experience chest pain, shortness of breath, an agonizing feeling that he's about to die. A special brain test known as a PET scan reveals in vivid color an area of heightened activity within the limbic system. With tranquilizer medication the "panic attack" subsides, leaving the executive embarrassed and frightened that he could have so suddenly "lost control."
- Epileptic discharges deep within the limbic system are detected in a thirty-five-year-old man charged with murder. He claims that he cannot recall the murder. Witnesses state that the man suddenly broke into a violent rage during which the murder occurred. Did epilepsy make him lose control? A psychiatrist is prepared to testify that it did on the basis of an electroencephalogram showing epileptic discharges in the anterior temporal lobe.

In the 1950s neurosurgeons discovered that if parts of the limbic system are electrically stimulated during a brain operation, the patient will experience fear and panic. Specific chemicals can cause the same reaction in certain individuals. A patient given to panic attacks is hooked up to an intravenous feeder. Within a few minutes after starting an infusion of sodium lactate solution, a commonly administered fluid replacement, a limbic-based attack of sudden overwhelming fear takes over. Despite his best efforts the patient is unable to calm himself. But after the lactate solution is stopped and a tranquilizer administered, the limbic discharge subsides and the patient calms down.

Many brain scientists are convinced that the limbic system may also be responsible for sudden outbursts of rage followed by violence—the so-called episodic dyscontrol syndrome. Limbic involvement has not appeared in every such patient, but enough cases have turned up with limbic abnormalities to warrant the use of electroencephalograms and other neurologic tests in cases of seemingly inexplicable outbursts of violence.

These discoveries linking some cases of violence to electrical discharges in the limbic system have important implications for any comprehensive theory about human behavior. Emotions are not incidental and subsidiary to rational processes. Even at his or her most reasonable moments, and despite all best efforts to the contrary, a person remains strongly influenced by feelings and emotions. (Psychologist William James described the interpenetration of thought and feeling long before the limbic system was discovered in an aptly titled essay, "The Sentiment of Rationality.")

Our legal system, however, has yet to incorporate these new insights: the reasonable man standard continues to be stressed. But as Guido Calabresi, dean of Yale Law School, points out in his book *Ideals, Beliefs, Attitudes and the Law,* definitions of "reasonable" have varied according to different cultures. In Roman law it was *bonus paterfamilias,* "the good father of the family"; in England, "the man on the Clapham omnibus"—something like your typical subway rider. In the United States, a typical definition given by courts and commentators is "the man who takes the magazines at home and in the evening pushes the lawn mower in his shirtsleeves."

Common to all of these descriptions has been the ordinariness and predictability of the "reasonable" person. But in the last century two major developments have occurred that make those criteria less valid. The first was the work of Sigmund Freud, whose description of the unconscious suggested that forces outside a person's control could exert a powerful influence on behavior. The insanity defense, with all its ramifications and variations, is based on this premise. That's why psychiatrists and not criminologists have traditionally testified, frequently offering conflicting opinions, as to whether a defendant is responsible for his actions.

The second development, sociobiology, arrived in the 1970s. According to sociobiologists, selection pressures exerted by the natural and social environments favor one behavior over another. Many of those behaviors are genetically determined. Over the past two decades genetic factors have been found to exert a strong influence on such mental illnesses as schizophrenia and manic depression. These agents modify the expression of certain personality disorders, such as obsessions and compulsions, and even influence such normal personality traits, as shyness or extroversion. An individual's actions, reasonable or otherwise, are therefore considered within the context of genes, environment, and surrounding society.

Currently the neurosciences have provided even more dramatic information about the role played by the limbic system. Consider this description, written by the subject's psychiatrist, of a fifty-one-year-old man who suddenly went into a tantrum because his wife and children differed with him on a trivial family matter: "Rage would well up within him, and he would begin cursing at the top of his voice. The feeling was one of lack of control, and soon he would begin smashing windows, breaking up the furniture, putting his fist through the walls and doors. This could go on for hours. He was aware of what was happening but felt driven to continue."

Except for these rare episodes, this man is otherwise indistinguishable from other family men who work regularly in middle-management positions. Do his outbursts reflect some form of "temporary insanity"? Or is he a reasonable man who becomes temporarily *un*reasonable? Whatever the answer, his outbursts—diagnosed by his psychiatrist as episodes of limbic dysfunction—are notable for two qualities. Once aroused to fury, the man feels "driven to continue," and the episodes can "go on for hours."

Given what we now know of such cases, the logic of the reasonable man standard in the Bernhard Goetz case, or similar cases in the future, may be inherently flawed.

"We don't contend that the defendant had no cause for apprehension," said Assistant District Attorney Gregory Waples on the first day of the trial. He argued that Goetz, once aroused, should have been capable of stopping himself at one point. His firing of a second shot into one of the assailants, Darrell Cabey, after, as the prosecution has contended, the immediate threat was over, is crucial to the state's argument. "When [Goetz] fired that last shot," Waples said, "beyond the slightest doubt, Cabey was seated, helpless, doing nothing to threaten or menace Bernhard Goetz." Consequently, according to Waples, Goetz is open to the charge that he did not act as a reasonable person.

The prosecutor's logic is that once Goetz coolly discerned that he was out of danger, he should have calmed down, put away his gun, and awaited the arrival of the police.

Although this undoubtedly would have made things easier for Goetz, such expectations are neurologically unrealistic. Once aroused, the limbic system can become a directive force for hours, sometimes days, and can rarely be shut off as if by flipping a switch. The heart keeps pounding; harsh and labored breathing burns in the throat; fear is replaced by anger and, finally, murderous rage. At some point in this process memories for ongoing events may become permanently lost; false memories may be created as the frightened and enraged person repeatedly relives the violent act he committed in response to what he perceived as a threat to his life.

Consider Goetz's response to the question "Did you just shoot each one of these people just once?"

Goetz: "Well, you see that's why I . . . that's . . . that's one of the things that puzzles me. . . . Because you know what you're doing, you cannot do something and not know it. I mean, how could I do it and not know it? But if you can accept this, I was out of control, and that's . . . you know . . . but that's . . . that's . . . it's true. Maybe you should always be in control, but if you . . . if you put people in a situation where they're threatened with mayhem, several times, and then if . . . then if something happens, and if a person acts, turns into a vicious animal . . . That's not the end of the shooting. That's what

. . . It's not the end. I ran back to the first two, to make sure."

Is that what a *reasonable* person would do under such circumstances?

Lawyers and judges love to explore such questions, but I'm convinced that these are the wrong questions. They reflect an outmoded orientation that overemphasizes the intellect. Excluded are the deep and powerful emotional currents of fear, self-preservation, or territoriality that can surface in any one of us and overpower our ability to reason.

This may not be a pretty or elegant arrangement, but as long as our brain is organized the way it is, none of us should be too confident that we would remain completely reasonable if we perceived our life to be in imminent danger. This critical perception of threat isn't based on rationality. It's fueled by those limbic-derived emotions that have ensured the survival of our species.

Isn't it preferable, therefore, to face up courageously to these sometimes frightening and unpleasant realities? Shouldn't we stop pretending that questions such as those asked about Bernhard Goetz can be answered by courtroom speculations about how a reasonable person would have responded in his place?

To expect reasonable behavior in the face of perceived threat, terror, and rage is itself a most unreasonable expectation.

❦❦❦

Name ______________________________ Date ______________ Period ________

Chapter 3

The Fiction of the Reasonable Man

1. What is the function of the limbic system?

2. Explain the following statement: "Emotions are not incidental and subsidiary to rational processes."

3. Describe some of the insights sociobiology has contributed to our understanding of human behavior.

Name ____________________ Date ____________ Period ________

Chapter 3

The Fiction of the Reasonable Man

4. Do you think that limbic dysfunction—or, as the author put it, the "deep and powerful emotional currents of fear, self-preservation, or territoriality"—should be grounds for a legal defense? Why or why not?

5. Do you think you have ever experienced a limbic malfunction? If so, when? Did you feel in control of your actions?

The Secret Life of James Thurber

V. S. Ramachandran, M.D., Ph.D., and Sandra Blakeslee

Ramachandran's major areas of research are: cognitive neuroscience, behavioral neurology (the study of cognitive and perceptual deficits in human neurological patients), neural plasticity and "phantom limbs."

Is this a dagger which I see before me,
The handle toward my hand?
Come, let me clutch thee:
I have thee not, and yet I see thee still.
Art thou not fatal vision, sensible
To feeling as to sight? or art thou but
A dagger of the mind, a false creation,
Proceeding from the heat oppressed brain?
—WILLIAM SHAKESPEARE

When James Thurber was six years old, a toy arrow shot accidentally at him by his brother impaled his right eye and he never saw out of that eye again. Though the loss was tragic, it was not devastating; like most one-eyed people he was able to navigate the world successfully. But much to his distress, in the years after the accident his left eye also started progressively deteriorating so that by the time he was thirty-five he had become completely blind. Yet ironically, far from being an impediment, Thurber's blindness somehow stimulated his imagination so that his visual field, instead of being dark and dreary, was filled with hallucinations, creating for him a fantastic world of surrealistic images. Thurber fans adore "The Secret Life of Walter Mitty," wherein Mitty, a milquetoast of a man, bounces back and forth between flights of fantasy and reality as if to mimic Thurber's own curious predicament. Even the whimsical cartoons for which he was so famous were probably provoked by his visual handicap.

Thus James Thurber was not blind in the sense that you or I might think of blindness—a falling darkness like the blackest night sky, entirely devoid of moonlight and stars, or even a complete absence of vision—an unbearable void. For Thurber, blindness was brilliant, star-studded and sprinkled with pixie dust. He once wrote to his ophthalmologist:

> Years ago you told me about a nun of the middle centuries who confused her retinal disturbances with holy visitation, although she saw only about one tenth of the holy symbols I see. Mine have included a blue Hoover, golden sparks, melting purple blobs, a skein of spit, a dancing brown spot, snowflakes, saffron and light blue waves, and two eight balls, to say nothing of the corona, which used to halo street lamps and is now brilliantly discernible when a shaft of light breaks against a crystal bowl or a bright metal edge. This corona, usually triple, is like a chrysanthemum composed of thousands of radiating petals, each ten times as slender and each containing in order the colors of the prism. Man has devised no spectacle of light in any way similar to this sublime arrangement of colors or holy visitation.

Once, after Thurber's glasses shattered, he said, "I saw a Cuban flag flying over a national bank, I saw a gay old lady with a gray parasol walk right through the side of a truck, I saw a cat roll across a street in a small striped barrel. I saw bridges rise lazily into the air, like balloons."

Thurber knew how to use his visions creatively. "The daydreamer," he said, "must

Pp. 85- of *Phantoms in the Brain* by V. S. Ramachandran, M.D., Ph.D. and Sandra Blakeslee.

visualize the dream so vividly and insistently that it becomes, in effect, an actuality."

Upon seeing his whimsical cartoons and reading his prose, I realized that Thurber probably suffered from an extraordinary neurological condition called Charles Bonnet syndrome. Patients with this curious disorder usually have damage somewhere in their visual pathway—in the eye or in the brain—causing them to be either completely or partially blind. Yet paradoxically, like Thurber, they start experiencing the most vivid visual hallucinations as if to "replace" the reality that is missing from their lives. Unlike many other disorders, Charles Bonnet syndrome is extremely common worldwide and affects millions of people whose vision has become compromised by glaucoma, cataracts, macular degeneration or diabetic retinopathy. Many such patients develop Thurberesque hallucinations—yet oddly enough most physicians have never heard about the disorder. One reason may be simply that people who have these symptoms are reluctant to mention them to anyone for fear of being labeled crazy. Who would believe that a blind person was seeing clowns and circus animals cavorting in her bedroom? When Grandma, sitting in her wheelchair in the nursing home, says, "What are all those water lilies doing on the floor?" her family is likely to think she's lost her mind.

If my diagnosis of Thurber's condition is correct, we must conclude that he wasn't just being metaphorical when he spoke of enhancing his creativity with his dreams and hallucinations; he really *did* experience all those haunting visions—a car in a striped barrel did indeed cross his visual field, snowflakes danced and a lady walked through the side of the truck.

But the images that Thurber and other Charles Bonnet patients experience are very different from those that you or I could conjure up in our minds. If I asked you to describe the American flag or to tell me how many sides a cube has, you'd maybe shut your eyes to avoid distraction and conjure up a faint internal mental picture, which you'd then proceed to scan and describe. (People vary greatly in this ability; many undergraduates say that they can only visualize four sides on a cube.) But the Charles Bonnet hallucinations are much more vivid and the patient has no conscious control over them—they emerge completely unbidden, although like real objects they may disappear when the eyes are closed.

I was intrigued by these hallucinations because of the internal contradiction they represent. They seem so extraordinarily real to the patient—indeed some tell me that the images are more "real than reality" or that the colors are "supervivid"—and yet we know they are mere figments of the imagination. The study of this syndrome may thus allow us to explore that mysterious no-man's-land between seeing and knowing and to discover how the lamp of our imagination illuminates the prosaic images of the world. Or it may even help us investigate the more basic question of how and where in the brain we actually "see" things—how the complex cascade of events in the thirty-odd visual areas in my cortex enables me to perceive and comprehend the world.

Name ______________________ Date ______________ Period ________

Chapter 4

The Secret Life of James Thurber

1. The author says that James Thurber was not blind in the sense that we think of blindness. How did Thurber's blindness differ?

2. What is Charles Bonnet syndrome?

Name ______________________ Date ______________ Period ________

Chapter 4

The Secret Life of James Thurber

3. Why do many people with Charles Bonnet syndrome not tell their doctors?

4. In what ways is experiencing Charles Bonnet syndrome like feeling a phantom limb?

The Educated Heart

Daniel Goleman

Daniel Goleman is the author of Emotional Intelligence *(Bantam, 1995) and* Working with Emotional Intelligence *(Bantam, 1998). He is cochairman of the Consortium for Research on Emotional Intelligence in Organizations, which is based at Rutgers University's Graduate School of Applied Professional Psychology in Piscataway, New Jersey.*

Across the Country, Schoolchildren Are Starting to Be Taught Such Skills as Empathy and Conflict Resolution in Order to Lessen Crime, Teenage Pregnancy, and Other Problems.

Today all the second-graders in Dawn DeNuzzo's class have the fidgets. But as DeNuzzo starts a video, a mesmeric calm settles over the room. The second-graders gaze at the screen, rapt in a dramatization of Krista's missing marker.

Krista sees that her deskmate, Nicole, is using an orange marker just like the lost one. "You stealer!" Krista says angrily, grabbing for the marker.

Indignant, Nicole yells back, "I did not!"

The two girls glower at each other as the scene fades.

Then the scene replays, this time with Krista pausing to ask politely if that's her missing marker.

Nicole replies, "No, I just got these new markers for my birthday." She adds sweetly, "But I just finished using it, and you can borrow it now."

Krista, placated, grumbles, "I just hate it when I lose things."

With that denouncement, the scene fades to a schoolmarmish announcer who underlines the lessons: Ask questions and listen. You can work it out without fighting. Next a slogan flashes on the screen: "Use your words"—shorthand for a crucial concept, "Use your words, not your fists."

As a snappy musical jingle comes up "WE can work it OUT, WE can work it out together!"—the second-graders spontaneously sing along. For all their undivided attention, the video may as well have been "The Lion King." A little boy pleads, "Can we see it again?"

Briskly, DeNuzzo picks up the momentum where the video left off: "What did the girls do to work it out?"

Leah's hand shoots up. "They asked questions."

"That's right," DeNuzzo beams. "They asked questions and talked it over instead of fighting. What are some things they could do that would make it better or worse? Call names?"

"Worse!" a chorus comes back.

"Refuse to talk to the person?"

"No—worse!"

"Try to understand how the person feels?"

"Better!"

This catechism of consequences, of thinking things over before acting, is part of a new approach to learning: an education of the heart. In classes like these throughout the New Haven, Connecticut, public-school system and in dozens of other pilot programs throughout the country, children are being given an education in what is being called "emotional literacy"—lessons in empathy and impulse control, in recognizing and handling feelings, and in just getting along.

This focus on the emotional fabric of students' lives is a radical departure: It puts in the

Daniel Goleman, *Common Boundary,* Nov/Dec 1995, pp. 22–30. Reprinted from the November/December 1995 issue of *Common Boundary,* 5272 River Road, Suite 650, Bethesda, MD 20816. Reprinted with author's permission.

foreground what is determinedly ignored in most American classrooms and relegated to trips to the principal's office for discipline or, for those too unruly, to "special ed" classes. Emotional literacy reinvents education, expanding the schools' mission to include essential lessons in the human skills children need for life. And it has come not a moment too soon: Our society is in the throes of social crises, with young people the most susceptible victims.

These crises can be read in statistics like those that identify the 1990s as having the highest juvenile arrest rate for violent crimes ever. The number of teen arrests for forcible rape has doubled over the previous two decades, and teen murder rates have quadrupled, mostly due to an increase in shootings. During those same two decades, the suicide rate for teenagers tripled, as did the number of children under 14 who were murder victims.

More, and younger, teenage girls are getting pregnant. As of 1993, the birth rate among girls 10 to 14 had risen steadily for five years in a row—some call the phenomenon "babies having babies"—as have the rate of teen pregnancies and peer pressure to have sex. The rate of venereal disease among teenagers has tripled over the last three decades.

If the focus shifts to African American youth, especially in the inner city, the figures become utterly bleak—all higher by far, sometimes doubled, sometimes tripled or more. For example, heroin and cocaine use among white youth climbed about three times over the two decades before the 1990s; for African American youth, it jumped 13 times the rate of 20 years before.

While headlines impress this gloomy picture on our collective awareness, we've missed a subtler, more telling story. Longitudinal studies show that specific social and emotional deficits raise the risk that a child will eventually develop such problems:

- Researchers in Montreal found that boys who are highly impulsive in kindergarten are three times more likely than others to be in trouble for fighting and to have a criminal record as teenagers.
- Impulsive grade-school girls, by contrast, don't become violent; according to a 1994 Portland, Oregon, study, they get pregnant as teenagers at about three times the rate of their peers.
- Gloria Leon of the University of Minnesota found that girls who at 10 years old are confused about the difference between anger, boredom, depression, and hunger are at a much higher risk of reacting to their emotional storms in relationships by developing the symptoms of eating disorders by early adolescence.
- Children who in grade school have what amounts to social dyslexia—misreading interpersonal cues—end up lonely and socially rejected. Steven Asher of the University of Illinois at Urbana found that they have three times the rate of dropping out of school as do their more socially adept peers.

The bad news is that such deficiencies are growing worse among American children. Using a representative national sample of thousands of children rated by their parents and teachers in the mid-1970s and then in the late '80s, Thomas Achenbach of the University of Vermont showed that over the intervening 13 years children had gotten worse on 42 indicators of social and emotional competence, including loneliness, sulking, listlessness, overdependence, fearfulness and worry, feeling unloved, nervousness, sadness and depression, fidgeting, difficulty paying attention, daydreaming, acting without thinking, lying and cheating, arguing, meanness, demanding attention, disobedience, moodiness and hot tempers. The only item that children had improved on was liking team sports better.

The underlying decay in children's emotional bedrock—and its role in putting them at peril—is why the New Haven schools turned to emotional literacy. In a direct challenge to much pedagogical orthodoxy, their strategy is to use the tensions and traumas of children's lives as the topic of the day. Teachers speak to real issues—envy, hurt feelings over being left out, anger at put-downs, and disputes that could escalate into schoolyard battles. Instead of talking about the compelling dramas of their lives only with a best friend or not at all, nursing emotional wounds with tears in the night, children are helped to deal with them openly and intelligently.

The New Haven schools are early harbingers of a revolutionary idea that is quietly spreading coast to coast. Names for these classes are innocuous, ranging from "social development" to "life skills" to "social and emotional learning." Some, referring to Harvard University psychologist Howard Gardner's idea of multiple intelligences, use the term "personal intelligences." These bland names give little sense of the dramatic educational vision they embody: schooling the heart along with the head.

The goal is to raise the level of social and emotional competence in children as part of their regular education—not just as something taught remedially to those who falter and get identified as "troubled" but as a set of skills and understandings essential for every child.

Only recently has there been a comprehensive theory to explain why this approach makes sense. The skills these courses build come under the rubric of "emotional intelligence," a term coined in 1990 by two psychologists, Peter Salovey of Yale University and John Mayer, now at the University of New Hampshire. It refers to the basic competencies of the human heart: knowing what you are feeling, being able to manage those feelings well, being able to delay impulse, maintaining hope and optimism despite setbacks, empathizing and taking others' perspectives, handling emotions in relationships, and interacting harmoniously. (See, "THE FUNDAMENTALS OF EMOTIONAL INTELLIGENCE.")

When it comes to handling the perils that children in the 1990s routinely face in life—and to turning back the tides of the social problems that besiege them—these skills are crucial, far more to the point than having a high IQ. As we all have seen, people of intellectual brilliance who lack these human traits can be extraordinarily poor pilots of their lives, especially when it comes to handling people and their own emotions. What's needed is emotional balance and social artfulness.

Take empathy, for instance. Psychologist Robert Rosenthal of Harvard University has found that there is virtually no relationship between people's IQ and their ability to "read" tone of voice or facial expression—the prime channels of emotion. Empathy, the source of caring and compassion, is a faculty developed in attunement between parent and child. This attunement lets a child know that her emotions are being met with recognition, that they are accepted and reciprocated. The countless repeated moments of attunement—or misattunement—between parent and child shape the emotional expectations children bring to their close relationships throughout life.

The natural unfolding of empathy can be seen in infants virtually from the day they were born. At first, infants show distress when another infant cries. They may crawl off to their mothers to be comforted—the other baby's distress is no different from their own. But by age one they start to try to comfort the other, a compassionate response that is almost universal among toddlers by age two. The exception is children who have suffered extreme neglect or severe abuse. For them, the trauma they have undergone puts them in danger of the extinction of empathy. Such preschoolers, for instance, are most apt to respond to a crying playmate with anger and pummeling fists instead of sympathy and attempts to help.

This damaged empathy may add to the risk that a child will follow the prototypical life trajectory that leads to criminal violence. That arc, longitudinal data show, begins with children who are already aggressive and hard to handle in the first and second grade and whose troublemaking adds to the difficulties they have as students. By fourth or fifth grade, these kids—now seen by peers as bullies and by teachers as "difficult"—are friendless and starting to fail school.

Lacking acceptance by their playmates, they gravitate to other social outcasts between fourth and ninth grade, and to a life of defying the rules—and the law. Over these years they show a fivefold increase in truancy, drinking, and drug-taking. In the high-school years they typically drop out and drift toward petty crime, eventually forming the core of youths arrested for violent crime.

Another factor in a youth's inclination toward such a life pattern is the fundamental emotional ability of resisting impulse. The Latin root of the word "emotion" means "to move outward"; all emotions, by their very nature, embody one or another impulse to act. Those who drift toward crime are among the children who are most impulsive.

In a test of the role of impulsive control in life, Stanford University researchers gave four-year-olds the "marshmallow test"—putting a marshmallow in front of them and telling them they could either have it now or wait several minutes and have two marshmallows later. Those who grabbed for the marshmallow grew into teenagers who were easily upset, prone to arguments and fights, and still unable to resist impulse very well. Those who had resisted temptation at age four were, as adolescents, better able to cope with the frustrations of life, more successful at school, and better able to put off gratification in pursuit of their goals.

Both empathy and impulse control are the roots of two other crucial strains in character: will and compassion. These later traits are among the elements of emotional intelligence that make for a good spouse, colleague, parent, or neighbor—in short, a decent human being.

While some people—notably Charles Murray and Richard Herrnstein in their book, THE BELL CURVE—argue that IQ cannot be changed and thus represents an unbendable limitation on a child's life potential, the good news from classrooms in emotional literacy is that children can learn to master emotional skills like empathy and impulse control.

The New Haven program covers the gamut of such emotional and social skills. In a fifth-grade class at the Troup Middle School, today's lesson is on identifying emotions. Being able to name feelings, in order to better distinguish among them, is a keystone of emotional intelligence. Last night's assignment was to bring in pictures from a magazine of a person's face and to name what emotion the face displays and how you can tell that the person is having those feelings.

After collecting the assignment, teacher Joyce Andrews lists the feelings on the board—sadness, worry, excitement, happiness, and so on—and launches into a fast-paced repartee with her students designed to expand their vocabulary for talking about feelings, thereby rendering the feelings less confusing.

As she adds "frustration" to the list on the board, Andrews asks, "How many people ever felt frustrated?" Every hand shoots up. "How do you feel when you're frustrated?"

The answers come in a cascade:

"Tired."

"Confused."

"You can't think right."

"Anxious."

Andrews asks, "When might you feel anxious?"

"When you wake up Christmas morning and want to see what you got," says a boy.

As "aggravation" is added to the list, Andrews says, "I know that one—when does a teacher feel aggravated?"

"When everyone is talking," a girl offers, smiling.

Without missing a beat, Andrews passes out a mimeographed work sheet. Along one column are faces of boys and girls, each displaying one of six basic emotions—happiness, sadness, anger, surprise, fear, disgust—and a description of the facial muscle activity underlying each. For fear, the description reads: "The mouth is open and drawn back; the eyes are open and the inner corners go up; the eyebrows are raised and drawn together; there are wrinkles in the middle of the forehead."

While the children read through the sheet, expressions of fear, anger, surprise, or disgust float over their faces as they imitate the pictures and read the facial-muscle recipes for each emotion. It's an elementary lesson in connecting a name with a feeling and connecting the feeling with the expression that matches it—a lesson that might seem so obvious that it needn't be taught. Yet it can serve as an antidote to surprisingly common lapses in emotional literacy. Schoolyard bullies, for instance, often strike out in anger because they misinterpret neutral messages and expressions as hostile.

The lesson comes straight from the work of Paul Ekman, an eminent emotions researcher and specialist on facial expression. It is taught in every college introductory psychology course—and virtually never in grade school.

Emotional intelligence, along with the emotional-literacy courses that seek to instill it, suggests a new and expanded role for psychology in society. By guiding the hands that shape our children in school, psychologists have created what amounts to an innovative program in primary prevention, inoculating children against the deficits that put them at risk for a host of problems, from depression and eating disorders to family violence and substance abuse.

These emotional-literacy courses have a remote root in the "affective education" movement of the 1960s. One of the first such courses, the "Self Science" curriculum at the Nueva Learning Center in Hillsborough, California, was designed by Karen Stone-McCown, who had gotten her training as an educator at the University of Massachusetts, at the time a hotbed of affective education.

The theory behind affective education was that psychological issues were more deeply learned if they involved an immediate experience of what was being taught conceptually. But emotional literacy turns the idea of affective education inside out: Instead of using affect to educate, it educates affect itself.

More immediately, most emotional-literacy courses and the momentum for their spread come from an ongoing series of school-based prevention programs, each targeting a specific problem: teen smoking, drinking or drug abuse, pregnancy, dropping out, and most recently, violence.

Karol DeFalco supervises the emotional-literacy curriculum in elementary and middle schools throughout New Haven. DeFalco tells how, in the late 1980s, with rates of dropouts, pregnancies, and drug use skyrocketing, the then-superintendent of New Haven's schools called together about 50 people, including several Yale psychologists, to come up with solutions.

"It turned out it didn't matter which specific problem a kid ended up with," DeFalco explains. "They all shared a core of deficits, including being poor at impulse control, at solving problems in their lives, at managing stress and emotions like anger, and in empathy and cooperation. So this curriculum was designed to help build these skills."

The rationale was buttressed by a national consortium of educators and psychologists organized by the W. T. Grant Foundation. Their mandate was to assess the proliferating programs for schools spawned as part of successive "wars" on violence, drugs, and other problems that plagued so many schools like New Haven's. After careful evaluation, the consortium concluded that a great number of these programs had little or no impact; some even made things worse.

But there were standouts here and there, all of which shared certain features: They were taught over many years rather than as one-shot lessons; they repeated basics throughout the grades in ways that were appropriate to students' changing comprehension; they emphasized the school as a community, tightening bonds to families and neighborhoods; and they inculcated the same core set of emotional and social skills as in the New Haven program, such as self-awareness, self-control, empathy, and cooperation.

With these principles in mind, a team of Yale psychologists patched together a curriculum, borrowing from a few of the better programs and creating lessons where none existed. The result is a methodical schooling in emotional intelligence that makes the approach unique. It starts in the earliest grades with exercises designed to help children recognize and name their feelings and what has caused them—like sitting in a circle and saying how they feel and why—and starting to think through the alternatives for handling those feelings. Starting in fourth grade, training in empathy, impulse control, and anger management is added to the mix.

By seventh grade, the program includes social problem solving, communications skills, stress management, handling relationships, and self-control. In eighth grade, the unit is part of mathematics, with an emphasis on self-monitoring and self-management—that is, tracking feelings like the urge to procrastinate and staying focused on the task at hand: math problems. In high school, the lessons in self-control, stress management, conflict resolution, and the like become increasingly sophisticated. All through the years these lessons are blended with more pointed ones on topics such as AIDS prevention, drug abuse, and teen pregnancy.

Emotional literacy is not a panacea for every problem facing children of the inner cities or those who haunt suburban shopping malls, but it seems to be making a decided difference. The best answers to how MUCH of a difference come from well-designed comparisons in a handful of pilot programs that are testing curriculums like New Haven's. The results read like a reversal of the emotional malaise documented in the University of Vermont evaluation of children by their parents and teachers: Children in emotional-literacy courses become better at recognizing feelings and understanding their causes, at tolerating frustration and managing anger, and at handling stress and calming themselves. They become more empathic and better at listening and taking another's perspective. They become less impulsive, depressed, and anxious. They get better at solving problems in relationships, setting disputes, and cooperating.

Another benefit has been a change in the school atmosphere. Students feel more positively about their schools and teachers. There are fewer fights, classroom disruptions, and suspensions. What's more, children can pay attention better and stay focused on the task at hand. Such students, of course, are easier to teach—one reason that teachers are enthusiastic. Finally, these students' achievement scores improve: It seems that when the heart is more at peace, the head is clearer.

Another way to tell the difference that emotional-literacy courses have made is to turn to the students themselves. Toni, 12 years old, testifies: "Someone said this girl wanted to fight me. I thought she was my friend, but they told me she was going to get me in a corner after school. So I went to the girl, and I asked why she said that stuff. And she said she never did. So we never had a fight."

The story seems innocuous enough, except that Toni has already been expelled from another school for fighting. It is no small victory for her to engage an apparent adversary in a constructive way rather than jumping to an angry confrontation. In the past she has attacked first, asked questions later—or not at all.

It is in the quiet accumulation of such small miracles, like this elusive "event"—a fight that did not happen—that emotional literacy has its most telling impact. As the 16th-century Dutch humanist Erasmus wrote, "The great hope of a nation lies in the proper education of its youth." In our day, a proper education may just come to mean one that includes the heart as well as the head.

Name ______________________________ Date ______________ Period ________

Chapter 5

The Educated Heart

1. Define the term "emotional literacy."

2. According to the article, is the ability to empathize and to read facial expressions related to a person's IQ?

3. The article suggests that "deficiencies" in empathic ability can be traced back to and predicted from childhood. How might this be useful in treating aggressive tendencies?

Name ________________ Date ________ Period ______

Chapter 5

The Educated Heart

4. What are the components of an effective emotional literacy program?

5. Have you ever participated in a course or an activity in which it was required that you share your feelings? Describe some potential problems that might arise when sharing personal feelings is "mandatory."

Sleepy Teenagers

Stanley Coren

Dr. Stanley Coren is a psychologist who has appeared on Dateline NBC and Good Morning America. (He is also an expert dog trainer who has written several books on the subject.)

In *The Winter's Tale,* Shakespeare has one of his characters comment, "I would there were no age between ten and three-and-twenty, or that youth would sleep out the rest; for there is nothing in the between but getting wenches with child, wronging the ancientry, stealing and fighting." Obviously, adolescents do not "sleep out" this period of their lives. In fact, current evidence suggests that adolescents may be an extremely sleep-deprived group. Some researchers even suggest that some of the impulsive, irresponsible, and unthinking behavior often seen at this age may be a consequence of this lack of sleep.

Between the ages of 6 and puberty (let's call it 12), the total amount of sleep children get shows a steady decline. While the 6-year-old may be getting 10 or 11 hours of sleep, the 12-year-old, about to enter adolescence, is typically getting 8½ hours of sleep a night. Children shorten their sleep time by extending their activities into the night. Some of these activities might be related to school, such as homework or studying; however, many are social or recreational in nature. Children tend to fill their evenings with television, listening to music, game playing, and socializing with friends (either in person or over the telephone). In other words, these children are doing exactly what their parents do. They are allowed to push back their bedtimes but are still committed to getting up early. After all, their schedule is locked into the beginning of the schoolday in the same way that their parents' wakening is fixed by the start of their workday. As the American writer James A. Baldwin put it, "Children have never been very good at listening to their elders, but they have never failed to imitate them."

Unfortunately, adopting the shortened sleep length that adults have is not a good idea for teenagers, either physically or psychologically. We find many individuals in later childhood showing patterns of thinking and acting, as well as variations in mood, that are common for people who are carrying a sleep debt. Laboratory research by Drs. Mary A. Carskadon and William Dement suggests that 10 hours of sleep are needed to fulfill the sleep needs of 12-year-olds. In fact, 10 hours of sleep may also be a fair estimate of the requirements of older adolescents as well.

It is in adolescence that we begin to see real evidence of sleep debt in children. From age 10 to 18 we see a steady pushing back of the time at which young people go to bed. It is not unusual for a 10-year-old to go to bed at 9 P.M. while the 18-year-old delays this until 1:30 A.M. on a weekday night. Some of this delay is due to the increasing demands from schoolwork and extracurricular activities on the adolescent's time, but some comes from the fact that additional time is often spent in working at a part-time job, either for luxury items and entertainment or for more vital purposes such as tuition and school expenses. There is evidence that teenagers who work more than 20 hours a week have very high levels of daytime sleepiness because of the inevitable lack of sleep.

There is a social factor that leads to sleep debt in teenagers as well. While most adults sleep longer on weekends in order to try to make up their sleep loss, many teenagers actually sleep less. Teenagers will often use the weekends for long nights of social activity. Although they might sleep late the morning after a night out, the actual amount of time spent asleep may be less than they get during the school week. This means that on Monday morning, when the alarm goes off, a teenager's sleep debt may actually be larger than it was on Friday. With this pattern of behavior the average teenager can build up a sizable sleep debt over the school year.

Sleep debt is more than a minor problem for teenagers. There have now been several large surveys of sleep habits for this age group, and one consistent finding is that more than half the teenagers studied wish that they had more time for sleep. There is evidence that during vacation periods, especially when away from home and in settings where social pressures for late night activities are reduced, teenagers revert to a sleep pattern in which they commonly sleep between 10 and 11 hours each day. This sleep duration seems to be much more consistent with estimates of their actual sleep requirements. On their usual sleep diet at home during the school year, most teenagers report bouts of sleepiness during the day. Teenagers also show periodic reductions in their alertness and their performance levels in tasks that require focused attention, precise movements, memory, problem solving, and other cognitive skills. These problems are frequently associated with times when the adolescent reaches a level of sleepiness in which he or she begins to have brief, unpredictable microsleeps, such as the afternoon low point in the daily circadian cycle. During these microsleeps the person simply slips, without any warning, into a sleep state for periods of a few seconds up to several minutes. An example of this comes from Alonzo, a 17-year-old high school junior:

I was sitting in my history class, with my notebook open and my pencil out, the way that I always do. This class is always hard 'cause it starts right after lunch and I'm tired then. That day Mr. G. was talking about taxes or something during the time when America was still an English colony. He was saying something about whisky and Pennsylvania, which wasn't too clear to me. The next thing I know, everybody is standing up. It took me a minute to figure out that class was over. I didn't hardly remember it starting. I looked at my notes for the class. I had written only two words: "Whisky Revolution." It freaked me a little. I knew I was tired and all that, but this was like just being unconscious.

One of the major signs of a teenager's sleep debt is the difficulty the parents have in waking him or her. While preadolescent children tend to wake up spontaneously in the morning and seem eager to start the day, adolescents and college students often need several reminders and prodding. The following solution to the problem of awakening is typical of college students:

Especially when I have a test in the morning, I really need more than one alarm clock. I set the clock-radio alarm next to the bed and make it loud. Then I set this world-class loud wind-up alarm on the dresser all the way across the room. I set it for 15 minutes later. I sleep through the clock-radio alarm a lot, but I have to get out of bed to turn the other alarm off or it will wake everybody in the house. That usually wakes me.

One story from a parent's viewpoint comes from the father of a college student:

Jeff had slept through one of his chemistry lab quizzes and was worried about doing it again. So he says to me, "Dad, you got to make sure I'm awake tomorrow because we've got another lab quiz. Just give me a good shake, and if I'm not awake kick me out of bed." So the next morning I go in, and he's like dead to the world. So I shake him, but he just makes noises. Finally, I got frustrated, so I grabbed his mattress by these little handles sewn on the sides and I flipped him right out of bed and onto the floor. "You up?" I asked him. "Yeah, Dad, I'm up," he says. So then I go off to work. When I get home that night, he's really angry at me. "Why didn't you stop and make sure I was up?" he asks. "I slept through the damn quiz again." So I say to him, "I rolled you onto the floor and you said you were awake." And he says to me, "You should have stayed and made sure I was awake. I always lie when I'm asleep!"

The common difficulty noted by parents in rousing their teenage offspring is one clear sign that they are not getting enough sleep. It may also be a sign that teenagers are suffering from a shift in their internal clocks. Dr. Mary A. Carskadon of Brown University has data that suggests that teenagers may have a *phase advance,* meaning that their circadian clock wants them to get up later and go to sleep later than most adults. A child's clock pattern seems to make a sharp change at around the time of puberty, and then it continues through to the 20s. In effect, teenagers become more like owls—happiest in the evening hours. One solution to the circadian shift in adolescence would be to shift the hours of high school so that the school day starts later and ends later.

Making changes in educational schedules to accommodate the internal timers of adolescents makes sense educationally. However, it is difficult to fit such changes into an already complex schedule of athletic and other after-school activities. Such changes would also conflict with the life rhythms of the adult world. In addition, some people feel that making such changes would be equivalent to "coddling" teenagers rather than forcing them to meet their responsibilities, which obviously include complying with educational schedules.

Some college administrators have now become aware of the problems associated with this pattern of teenage behavior. One of them reported that many classes that are held early in the mornings have absenteeism rates as high as 40 percent, even when the classes are taught by popular instructors. One university department head told me the following:

For a while we recommended that required first- and second-year courses not be held in the first two or three hours of the day but should be pushed off until the afternoon. At least then we know that most students are prone to be awake and on campus. Unfortunately, this led to a space crisis. We didn't have enough lecture halls for the large first-year classes that were all trying to squeeze into the afternoon. When a committee came up with a suggestion that we build more lecture theaters for this purpose, the Provost exploded: "If they [the students] *can't get the hell out of bed in time to attend classes, then that is their problem. The next thing I expect is that the committee will be asking that we install cots in the lecture halls for the comfort of students who like to sleep in class!"*

Perhaps one of the aspects of adolescent sleep that is most important for later life is the fact that teenagers are developing the adult attitude toward sleep, that is, the attitude that whenever anything interesting or important comes up that requires more time, the way you find that time is by cheating on sleep. This kind of behavior in college students is reflected in expressions like "burning the midnight oil" or "pulling an all-nighter." These terms are usually applied to studying deep into the night before an exam or in order to finish a paper or other required project. Since school in adolescence is equivalent to employment in adulthood, the patterns of behavior teenagers develop toward work, leisure time, and sleep are usually carried over into their adult lives.

All-nighters are mostly the result of instances in which the student has simply put off doing required work or studying because there were more interesting or pressing activities to pursue. As the deadline grows closer, time must be stolen from somewhere to make up for the earlier procrastination. This usually means sacrificing sleep for an all-night work or study session. Students are rewarded for this effort in two ways: First, they are rewarded socially by friends and even by parents, who seem to admire such heroic efforts and often view the sleep loss involved as evidence that the student is committed, ambitious, energetic, or at least tough enough to take the stress. This reflects the attitude of society as a whole. The person who sleeps in is viewed as lazy while the person who goes without sleep is strong and to be admired. The second way in which the student is rewarded is by the actual results. At least for material that requires rote memorization (such as language courses, some aspects of history courses, and aspects of science courses that require learning labels for species, body parts, geological formations, and so forth), cramming all of the material into one extended night of study works—sort of. This kind of material can be held in memory despite the sleep loss, at least for a short while. Often it is retained for long enough to make it through the exam. Unfortunately, this material is soon lost from memory. In the absence of adequate sleep the memories do not "consolidate" (which is the technical term for being entered into our long-term memory storage). Long-term memory is virtually unlimited in capacity and relatively indestructible. Studies have shown that foreign words learned in a high school course but never again used can be remembered 50 years later if they made it into long-term memory when they were originally learned. Conversely, items that do not make it into long-term memory begin to fade and are quickly lost.

All-nighters are also not very effective in learning material that requires the student to solve complex logical problems or use "divergent thinking." Divergent thinking is important when we are trying to come up with creative solutions or when problem solving requires us to be flexible and try new approaches. There is a good deal of research that shows that it is these aspects of thinking that are lost most quickly following sleep loss. Thus, all-nighters might work for a course where students "spit back" memorized material, but when this material must be used to solve problems or discuss complicated issues or points of view, they are not very effective. This also means that if the student is going without sleep in order to finish a term paper and if this term paper is going to be graded on the basis of the quality and originality of thought, the all-nighter is really counterproductive. Papers produced during all-nighters often seem flat and uninspired and frequently show obvious gaps in logic and organization.

Despite evidence that losing sleep in order to study is not a productive strategy, it still seems to be admired and demanded by segments of our society. In fact, in some cultures the process has become quite institutionalized. In Japan, for example, students are under a lot of pressure to do well in the national college entrance exams. As part of what is viewed as "diligent studying," many students attend special schools known as *juku* after the regular schoolday is finished. These schools attempt to cram as much material into the students as possible. Following *juku,* the students are expected to go home and continue studying. It is not unusual for them to continue their study deep into the night. Students are often actually encouraged to reduce the amount of sleep they take nightly in order to study. A common expression many Japanese students have adopted as their motto is "Pass with four, fail with five"; the numbers refer to the number of hours of sleep the students take each night. If, as research shows, this process is not very useful as a strategy to produce good long-term retention of the learned material and if this sleep loss is actually reducing the quality of creative and original thinking in these students, why is it encouraged? Some cultural researchers have suggested that the Japanese system serves as a sort of initiation rite: by doing well on the exams, especially under these conditions, students prove to colleges and also to future employers that they have the stamina, ambition, and personal fortitude to take the pressure and still succeed.

Name ______________________ Date ______________ Period ________

Chapter 6

Sleepy Teenagers

1. What, according to the author, is a sleep debt and how is it created?

2. How does the social factor affect the sleep debt?

3. What are some symptoms or characteristics of a lack of sleep?

Name ______________________ Date ______________ Period __________

Chapter 6

Sleepy Teenagers

4. Why does the author warn against pulling "all-nighters" before important exams?

5. Some sleep experts have recommended shifting high school so that it starts later and ends later, in effect moving toward a more night-time centered schedule. Would this work for you? Why or why not? Do you think it would be practical?

On Responsibility and Punishment

John Staddon

John E. R. Staddon is the J. B. Duke Professor of Psychology, Professor of Zoology and Neurobiology. He has written many books on behavioral analysis including this 1995 excerpt from the Atlantic Monthly magazine.

The litany of social dysfunction is now familiar. The rates of violent crime are 40 percent higher than they were a decade ago; Americans kill and maim one another at per capita rates five to ten times as high as those of other industrialized nations: The rate of illegitimacy continues to climb. Tens of thousands of children have no fathers and no family members or close acquaintances who hold regular jobs; this pattern is now repeating into the second and third generations. Illiteracy is a big problem, and schools have so lost authority that the accepted response to armed pupils is to install metal detectors. Senator Daniel Patrick Moynihan, in a celebrated article, recently pointed out that we cope with social disintegration by redefining deviancy, so that crimes become "normal" behavior.

How did we arrive at this condition? There's no short answer, but I have increasingly come to believe that my own profession—psychology—bears a large part of the blame. The story began many years ago, when psychology defined itself as a science. Thus self-anointed, the discipline gained great prestige. People accepted with little demur prescriptions that would earlier have been condemned on moral grounds. Don't spank your child. Don't attempt to deter sexual exploration by young people—deterrence is probably bad and will certainly fail. Punishment is ineffective and should be replaced by positive reinforcement. Self-esteem is good, social stigma bad. It is not clear that this advice was all wrong. What is clear, and what I will show in this article, is that it was not based on science.

Some questions about behavior can be answered—either now or in the future—through the methods of science. How does visual perception work? What are the effects of different reward schedules? How accurate is memory for words and faces? What lighting conditions are best for different kinds of tasks? Which people are likely to succeed in which professions? Other questions, including apparently simple ones such as the value of some teaching techniques and the legitimacy of corporal punishment, cannot be answered by science, because they have consequences that go beyond the individual or far into the future. Corporal punishment and teaching methods affect not just the child but, eventually, the nature of society. Society cannot be the subject of experiments, and even if it could, the effects of social changes usually take decades or even centuries to play out. Hence we often cannot expect to get hard scientific answers to social questions.

Obviously, we need to separate those questions that belong in the domain of science from those that do not—to separate questions that can be answered definitively from those that cannot. Unfortunately, psychology as a profession tends to assume that all questions about human action fall within its domain and that all can eventually be answered with the authority of science—and this imperialism has gone largely unquestioned.

Psychologists and behavioral psychiatrists seem a diverse crew. At one end of the spectrum

The Atlantic Monthly, Feb 1995, v275, n2, p.88(6), © 1995, John Staddon, as first published in *The Atlantic Monthly.*

we have touchy-feelies who say things like "Any of us who were raised in the traditional patriarchal system have trouble relating because we've been 'mystified' to some degree by an upbringing that compels obedience and rules by fear, a raising that can be survived only by denial of the authentic self" (John Bradshaw). At the other we have the behaviorists, who say things like "In the scientific view . . . a person's behavior is determined by a genetic endowment traceable to the evolutionary history of the species and by the environmental circumstances to which as an individual he has been exposed" (B. F. Skinner).

Bradshaw and Skinner seem to agree on little. It may come as a surprise, therefore, to learn that psychological pundits from Bradshaw to Skinner agree on several important things. Almost all focus entirely on the individual. All reject what Bradshaw calls "fear," Skinner called "aversive contingency," and the rest of us call punishment. Nearly all psychologists believe that behavior is completely determined by heredity and environment. A substantial majority agree with Skinner that determinism rules out the concept of personal responsibility. This opposition between determinism and responsibility is now widely accepted, not just by behaviorists but by every category of mental-health professional, by journalists, by much of the public—and by many in the legal profession.

Behaviorism is the most self-consciously "scientific" of the many strands that make up psychology. Although somewhat overshadowed recently by cognitive psychology and other movements, behaviorism has had overwhelming influence during most of the short history of psychology. Consequently, when behaviorists have produced hard evidence in favor of beliefs already shared by other psychologists, the combined effect has always been decisive. I will describe just such a confluence in this article.

About moral positions, argument is possible. But about scientific facts there can be no argument. Skinner, and the behaviorist movement of which he was the head, delegitimized both individual responsibility and punishment. Responsibility was dismissed by philosophical argument. Punishment was ruled out not by moral opposition but by supposedly scientific laboratory results. Less science-oriented psychologists and psychiatrists have agreed that punishment is bad, but the reasons for their consensus are more complex, and have to do with the social function of psychotherapy. Nevertheless, for the majority of psychologists and psychiatrists, the facts established by the behaviorists have always constituted an unanswerable argument—especially if these have supported pre-existing beliefs. This "scientific" consensus has had a devastating effect on the moral basis of American society.

I will argue, first, that there is no opposition between behavioral determinism and the notion of individual responsibility, and second, that the scientific basis for blanket opposition to punishment as a legitimate social instrument—in the family, the school, the workplace, and the judicial system—is nonexistent. My focus is Skinnerian behaviorism because it is the area of psychology that has been most concerned with large social issues. But the key ideas have been carried forward by a much larger number of psychologists and psychiatrists who have never thought of themselves as behaviorists.

B. F. Skinner's 1971 best seller Beyond Freedom and Dignity contains his most concerted, and successful, attack on traditional methods of social control. Most psychotherapists, behaviorist and nonbehaviorist alike, have come to agree with the substance of Skinner's message: that punishment is bad and that the idea of individual responsibility is a myth. Skinner's argument is simply wrong. It will be a task for future sociologists to understand why such a bad argument received such ready assent.

Skinner contrasted the "prescientific" view that "a person's behavior is at least to some extent his own achievement" with the "scientific" view that behavior is completely determined by heredity and environment. The conventional view, he wrote, is that a person is free.

"He is autonomous in the sense that his behavior is uncaused. He can therefore be held responsible for what he does and justly punished if he offends. That view, together with its associated practices, must be re-examined when a scientific analysis reveals unsuspected controlling relations between behavior and environment."

What's wrong with this apparently judicious line of reasoning?

Freedom

Is man free? Well, as the professor used to say, it depends on what you mean by "freedom." The bottom line is that you're free if you feel free. Skinner's definition is simpler: to him, freedom was simply the absence of punishment ("aversive contingencies"). But we are all "punished" by gravity if we seek to disobey its rules. The punishment can sometimes be quite severe, as beginning cyclists and skaters can attest. Yet we don't feel unfree when we learn to skate or cycle. Punishment doesn't always abolish freedom—and freedom is not just the absence of punishment.

Skinner had another definition of freedom: absence of causation ("autonomous man"). This is an odd notion indeed. How can one ever prove the absence of causation? In science a conjecture like this is called a null hypothesis, and everyone accepts that such a thing is impossible to prove. We might prove the obverse, however: that people are unfree when their behavior is determined—that is to say, when it can be predicted. For example, suppose a rich and generous aunt offers her young niece a choice between a small sum of money and a large sum. In the absence of any contrary factors, the niece will doubtless pick the larger over the smaller. (Classical economics rests on the assumption that this will always be the choice made.) Can we predict the niece's behavior? Certainly. Is her behavior determined? Yes, by all the usual criteria. Is she unfree? She certainly doesn't feel unfree. People generally feel free when they follow their preferences, no matter how predictable those preferences may be. Behavior can be predicted in other contexts as well. Mathematicians predictably follow the laws of arithmetic, architects the laws of geometry, and baseball players the laws of physics. The behavior of all is determined; yet all feel free. Ergo, predictability—determinism—doesn't equal the absence of freedom, as Skinner proposes.

So even if we could predict all human behavior with absolute precision, this wonderful new science would have no bearing at all on the idea of freedom.

Punishment

There is another strand in Skinner's assault on traditional practices—his attack on punishment. He rejected punishment not because it's morally wrong but because it doesn't work. (W. H. Auden had no such doubts about punishment when remarked, "Give me a no-nonsense, down-to-earth behaviorist, a few drugs, and simple electrical appliances, and in six months I will have him reciting the Athanasian Creed in public.") Since everyone knows that some punishments sometimes work, you may be curious to hear how Skinner defended his position. His argument boils down to three points: punishment is ineffective because when you stop punishing, the punished behavior returns; punishment provokes "counterattack"; positive reinforcement is better. Let's look at each of these.

Punishment Is Ineffective. Well, no, it isn't. Common sense aside, laboratory studies with pigeons and rats (the basis for Skinner's argument) show that punishment (usually a brief electric shock) works very well to suppress behavior, as long as it is of the right magnitude and follows promptly on the behavior that is to be suppressed. If a rat gets a moderate shock when he presses a bar, he stops pressing it more or less at once. If the shock is too great, the rat stops doing anything; if the shock is too weak, he may still press the bar once in a while; if it's just right, he quits pressing but otherwise behaves normally. Does the punished behavior return when the punishment is withdrawn? That depends on the training procedure. An avoidance procedure called shock postponement, in which the rat gets no shock so long as he presses the bar once in a while, produces behavior that can persist indefinitely when the shock schedule is withdrawn. That is to say, the rat continues periodically to press the bar.

Punishment Provokes Counterattack. Sure: if a food-producing lever also produces shock, the rat will try to get the food without getting the shock. A famous picture in introductory-psychology texts is called "Breakfast in Bed." It shows a rat that learned in a shock-food experiment to press the lever while lying on his back, insulated by his fur from the metal floor grid. Skinner was right that rats, and people, try to beat a punishment schedule.

Positive Reinforcement Is More Effective. Not true. The effects of positive reinforcement also dissipate when the reinforcement is withdrawn, and there is no positive-reinforcement procedure that produces behavior as persistent as that produced by a shock-postponement schedule. Positive reinforcement also provokes counterattack. Every student who cheats, every gambler who rigs the odds, every robber and thief, shows the counterattack provoked by positive-reinforcement schedules.

There are other arguments on both sides, but the net conclusion must be that the scientific evidence is pretty much neutral in deciding between reward and punishment. Each has its advantages and disadvantages: punishment is better for suppressing behavior, positive reinforcement better for generating behavior, punishment tends to produce more-persistent behavior than rewards; and so on. If we wish to favor reward over punishment, we must make a moral, not a scientific, case.

Justice and Determinism

All this might be academic but for its impact on legal thinking. The opposition between determinism and responsibility, and the doubts cast on punishment, do seem to raise issues of justice. If the devil—or, at least, "my environment"—made me do it, surely I should be spared the rigors of just punishment (of dubious effectiveness in any case, according to psychologists). In the era of Lorena Bobbitt, Reginald Denny's attackers, and the Menendez brothers, this argument evidently strikes a receptive chord in the hearts of American juries.

Too bad, because the argument is false. I've already argued that behavior can be both determined (in the sense of predictable) and free. I'll argue now that the legal concept of personal responsibility is founded on this kind of predictability. Personal responsibility demands that behavior be predictable—not the opposite, as Skinner contended.

What is the purpose of judicial punishment? Legal scholars normally identify two purposes, retribution and deterrence. Retribution is a moral concept, which need not concern us here. But deterrence is a practical matter. Arguments about deterrence are clouded by ideology and the impossibility of deciding the issue by the methods of science. Nevertheless, there is a straightforward approach to deterrence that would much simplify a jury's task. The idea is that the purpose of legal punishment is to minimize the total amount of suffering in society—the suffering caused by crime as well as the suffering caused by punishment. The concept is simple: If thievery is punished by amputation, the level of thievery will be low but the level of suffering of thieves will be very high—higher, perhaps, than warranted by the reduction in theft. On the other hand, if murderers go free, the level of murder will be high and the ease of the killers will not balance the suffering of the rest. We may argue about how to measure suffering and how to assess the effect of a given level of legal punishment for a given crime, but the principle, which I call the social view of punishment, seems reasonable enough. It is consistent with the fundamental principle that government exists for the welfare of society as a whole, not for the good of any particular individual. Once they understand the argument, most people seem to agree that the social view of punishment is acceptable, although not, perhaps, the whole story. What people do not seem to realize is that this perfectly reasonable view is not opposed to determinism; it requires determinism.

From an objective point of view—the only legitimate point of view for science—"holding a man responsible" for his actions means nothing more than making him subject to punishment if he breaks the law. The social view of punishment assumes that people are sensitive to reward and punishment—that behavior is predictably subject to causal influences. If criminal behavior is predictably deterred by punishment, the justly punished criminal is less likely to disobey the law again, and serves as an example to other potential lawbreakers. This is the only objective justification for punishment. But if behavior were unpredictable and unaffected by "reinforcement contingencies"—if it were uncaused, in Skinner's caricature of freedom—there would be absolutely no point to punishment or any other form of behavioral control, because it would have no predictable effect. In short, legal responsibility requires behavioral determinism.

It is interesting to reflect that the objective case for personal responsibility rests entirely on the beneficial collective effects of just punishment (on minimizing the sum total of human suffering). It does not rest on philosophical notions of individual autonomy, or personal intent, or anything else at the level of the individual—other than normal susceptibility to reward and punishment. The idea that the law is somehow concerned with the mental state of the accused, rather than with the consequences of judicial action, has taken root because Skinner, like most other psychologists, focused almost exclusively on the individual.

If a person's "behavior is at least to some extent his own achievement," Skinner wrote, then he can be praised for success and blamed for failure. Since personal responsibility is a myth (he concluded), praise and blame are irrelevant. But if personal responsibility is defined as I have defined it, praise and blame need not—should not—be abandoned. In the social view, the use of praise and blame has nothing to do with the ontology of personal responsibility, the epistemology of intention, or whatnot. It has everything to do with reward and punishment (in other contexts Skinner admitted as much, at least with respect to praise). We praise good behavior because we wish to see more of it; we censure the criminal because we wish to see less crime. Praise and blame are perhaps the strongest incentives available to society. By giving them up, Skinner gave up our best tools for social order.

It is extraordinary that Skinner seems to have missed the connection between determinism and the sanctions imposed by the legal system. He spent his life studying how the behavior of animals is determined by the conditions of reward and punishment. He and his students discovered dozens of subtle and previously unsuspected regularities in the actions of reward and punishment. Yet he failed to see that the system of rewards and punishments imposed by society works in much the same way as his reinforcement schedules.

Remarkably, law and science seem to agree on the social view of punishment. Only when punishment is likely to be completely ineffective as a deterrent does the law limit its use. If the criminal is insane, or if injury was the unintended result of actions whose harmful outcome was unforeseeable, no guilt is attached to the perpetrator and no punishment is meted out—presumably because punishment can play no role in preventing a recurrence of the crime or the injury. There is surprising congruence between the legal concept of responsibility and the function of punishment as a deterrent. "Guilt" is established not so much by the act as by the potential of punishment to deter the act.

The "Victim" Defense: What Should the Jury Do?

These arguments greatly simplify a jury's task. Jurors have no need to puzzle through philosophical questions about intent or knowledge of right and wrong. Nor do they need to ask whether criminal behavior was determined by the defendant's history. (The scientific answer will almost always be yes, because almost all behavior is determined.) History is not the point. The point is, Did the defendant know that his actions would have an illegal outcome? And if he had known in advance of the act that sure punishment would follow, would he still have acted as he did? If the criminal would have been deterred by the prospect of punishment, the social view says, then he should be punished. Did the Menendez brothers know that their actions would result in the death of their parents? Presumably yes. If they had known that those acts would result in severe punishment (life in prison or death), would they have acted nevertheless? Probably not. Verdict: Guilty. On the other hand, if the jury had reason to believe that the defendants' history was so horrific that they would have murdered even in the face of certain punishment, then some other verdict (which might still involve removing these damaged men from society) would be appropriate.

The Proper Role of Psychology

The social view of punishment is as far as psychology can go toward prescribing social policy. Given a certain set of values, psychology may help us decide what system of rewards and punishments will be helpful in promoting them. But the social view of reward and punishment does not by itself prescribe social policy. Our value system, our morality, plays a legitimate role in measuring suffering, in evaluating known outcomes, and in judging the rightness or wrongness of particular rewards and punishments. We're less moved by the plight of the disappointed thief who breaks open an empty safe than by the suffering of a mugging victim, for example. Psychology can tell us a little (only a little, since we don't do such experiments on human beings) about the effects on individuals of corporal punishment versus the effects of a jail term; it cannot tell us whether corporal punishment is cruel or not. Social science can tell us that more people will be killed by guns if guns are freely available than if they are not; it cannot tell us whether the freedom to bear arms is an inalienable right. Psychology can tell us something about the extent of homosexuality in different cultures; it cannot tell us whether homosexuality is good, bad, or a matter of indifference. Psychology can also tell us that social opprobrium—Hester Prynne's A, blame, or the big red D some have proposed for drunk drivers—is often an effective deterrent. It cannot tell us whether such punishment is right or not. Scientific psychology, like all science, is amoral: it tells us what is or what might be—not what should be. Psychologists who offer more, promoters of the "authentic self" or punishment-free societies, are peddling not science but faith.

Name ______________________ Date ______________ Period ________

Chapter 7

On Responsibility and Punishment

1. What is behaviorism?

2. What three points does Skinner stress in his argument against punishment?

3. According to the author, what is the principal purpose of judicial punishment?

Name ______________________ Date ______________ Period __________

Chapter 7

On Responsibility and Punishment

4. Why does the social view of punishment depend upon the concept of determinism?

5. Do you think that punishment is an effective deterrent? Would you break a rule knowing for certain that you would be punished?

Chapter 8 Information Processing and Memory

It's Magical! It's Malleable! It's . . . Memory

Jill Neimark

Jill Neimark is a free lance researcher and writer. This article first appeared in Psychology Today *in January 1995. In this article she discusses the theories of Elizabeth Loftus.*

We never know exactly why certain subjects—like certain people—claim us, and do not let us go. Elizabeth Loftus is a research psychologist who has devoted her life to the study of memory, its mystery and malleability. Of late, she has gained ingenious experiments, which have shown repeatedly that about 25 percent of individuals can be easily induced to remember events that never happened to them—false memories that feel absolutely real.

So it was something of a shock when, at a family gathering, an uncle informed the then 44-year-old Loftus that 30 years earlier, when her mother had drowned, she had been the one to discover the body in the pool. Loftus believed she had never seen her mother's dead body; in fact, she remembered little about the death itself.

Almost immediately after her uncle's revelation, "the memories began to drift back," she recalls in her recent book, *The Myth of Repressed Memory* (St. Martin), "like the crisp, piney smoke from evening camp fires. My mother, dressed in her nightgown, was floating face down. . . . I started screaming. I remembered the police cars, their lights flashing. For three days my memory expanded and swelled.

"Then, early one morning, my brother called to tell me that my uncle had made a mistake. Now he remembered (and other relatives confirmed) that Aunt Pearl found my mother's body." Suddenly Loftus understood firsthand what she had been studying for decades. "My own experiment had inadvertently been performed on me! I was left with a sense of wonder at the inherent credulity of even my skeptical mind."

Memory has become a lightning rod of late. This has been a time of fascinating, grisly stories—of recovered memories of satanic cults, butchered babies, and incest that have spawned church scandals, lawsuits, suicides, splintered families, murders, and endless fodder for talk shows. Three major books on the fallibility of memory were reviewed on the front page of the *New York Times Book Review* last spring, and three more were published this fall. The essential nature of memory, which ought by rights to be a scientific debate, has so galvanized the culture that laws have actually been revoked and repealed over it; in Illinois, for example, a law that bars people over 30 from filing lawsuits based on remembered abuse was repealed in 1992, and is now being reinstated.

Memory's ambiguities and paradoxes seem to have suddenly claimed us as they have claimed researchers for decades. This fascination cannot be explained away by the human need to memorialize the past—a need that expresses itself beautifully and indelibly in monuments like the Vietnam memorial or the AIDS quilt, and in projects like Steven Spielberg's ongoing documentary of holocaust survivors.

It's as if we've awakened, at the turn of the millennium, and realized that memory is the bedrock of the self—and that it may be perpetually shifting and terrifically malleable. That image of memory, whose river runs into tabloids and traumas, seems both terrifying and baptismal. If we can repress life-shaping events (such as sexual or physical abuse), or actually invent memories of events that never happened (from UFO abductions to rapes and murders), memory carries a power that promises to utterly reshape the self.

And so it's exciting news that in the past few years, scientists have begun to piece together a picture of memory that is stunning in its specifics:

- Sophisticated PET (positron emission tomography) scans can record the actual firing of the neurons that hold the pictures of our lives, and observe memory move like a current across the brain while it sleeps or wakes.
- How and where the brain lays down and consolidates memory—that is, makes it permanent—is yielding to understanding. As one researcher states, we are seeing "an explosion of knowledge about what parts of the brain are doing what."
- Hormones that help engrave the narrative of our lives into our cells have now been identified.
- Certain drugs block or enhance memory, and they may hold the key to preventing disorders as wide-ranging as Alzheimer's disease and posttraumatic stress disorder (PTSD).
- The well-known "fight-or-flight" response to stress can sear "indelible" memories into the brain.
- Memory is not a single entity residing in a single place. It is the likelihood that the pathway of neurons and connections an experience forges in the brain can be reactivated again. It involves multiple systems in the brain. The emotion associated with a memory, for example, is stored in a different place than the content of the memory itself.
- Some memories occur in a primitive part of the brain, unknown to conscious perception. That part functions "below" the senses, as it were. That is why individuals with brain damage can sometimes learn and remember—without knowing they do so.
- There is a growing understanding that an infant's early experience of emotional attachment can direct the nature and durability of childhood memories and the way they are stored in the brain.

Memory, it turns out, is both far more complex and more primitive than we knew. Ancient parts of the brain can record memory before it even reaches our senses—our sight and hearing, for instance. At the same time, "there are between 200 and 400 billion neurons in the brain and each neuron has about 10,000 connections," notes psychiatrist Daniel Siegel, M.D. "The parallel processing involved in memory is so complex we can't even begin to think how it works."

The one thing that we can say for certain is this: If memory is the bedrock of the self, then even though that self may seem coherent and unchanging, it is built on shifting sands.

Thirteen Ways of Looking at the Brain

Moments after being removed from the skull, the brain begins to collapse into a jelly-like mass. And yet this wet aspic of tissue contains a fantastic archeology of glands, organs, and lobes, all of which have their own specialized jobs. Much of this archeology is devoted to the complex tasks of memory.

But just what is memory? According to Nobel Prize-winning neuroscientist Gerald Edelman, Ph.D., author of *Bright Air, Brilliant Fire* (Basic Books), memory is the ability to repeat a performance—with mistakes. Without memory, life itself would never have evolved. The genetic code must be able to repeat itself in DNA and RNA; an immune cell must be able to remember an antigen and repeat a highly specific defense next time they meet; a neuron in the brain must be able to send the same signal each time you encounter (for example) a lion escaped from the local zoo. Every living system must be able to remember; but what is most dangerous and wonderful about memory is that it must occasionally make errors. It must be wrong. Mere repetition might explain the way a crystal grows but not the way a brain works. Memory classifies and adapts to our environment. That adaptation requires flexibility. The very ability to make mistakes is precious.

Now you can bravely step into the hall of mirrors that is memory. And though our words to describe this evanescent process are still crude and oversimplistic, here are a few tools to travel with:

Memory can be implicit or explicit. Implicit memory is involved in learning habits—such as riding a bicycle or driving a car. It does not require "conscious" awareness, which is why you can sometimes be lost in thought as you drive and find you've driven home without realizing it. Explicit memory is conscious, and is sometimes called declarative. One form of declarative memory is autobiographical memory—our ability to tell the story of our life in the context of time.

We often talk of memory storage and retrieval, as if memory were filed in a honeycomb of compartments, but these words are really only metaphors. If memory is the reactivation of a weblike network of neurons that were first activated when an event occurred, each time that network is stimulated the memory is strengthened, or consolidated. Storage, retrieval, consolidation—how comforting and solid they sound; but in fact they consist of electrical charges leaping among a vast tangle of neurons.

In truth, even the simplest memory stimulates complex neural networks at several different sites in the brain. The content (what happened) and meaning (how it felt) of an event are laid down in separate parts of the brain. In fact, research at Yale University by Patricia Goldman-Rakic, Ph.D., has shown that neurons themselves are specialized for different types of memories—features, patterns, location, direction. "The coding is so specific that it can be mapped to different areas . . . in the prefrontal region."

What is activating these myriad connections? We still don't know. Gerald Edelman calls this mystery "the homunculus crisis." Who is thinking? Is memory remembering us? "The intricacy and numerosity of brain connections are extraordinary," writes Edelman. "The layers and loops between them are dynamic, they continually change."

Yet the center holds. The master regulator of memory, the hub at the center of the wheel, is a little seahorse-shaped organ called the hippocampus. Like the rest of the brain, it is lateralized; it exists in both the right and left hemispheres. Without it, we learn and remember nothing—in fact, we are lost to ourselves.

The Seahorse and the Self

"He's 33 years old, and he never remembers that his father is dead. Every time he rediscovers this fact he goes through the whole grieving process again," Mark Gluck, Ph.D., a professor at the Center for Molecular and Behavioral Neuroscience at Rutgers University, says of M.P., a young man who lost his memory after a stroke six years ago. Gluck has been studying M.P. for several years. After his stroke, M.P. forgot that on that very morning he had proposed marriage to his girlfriend. "He can store no new information in his long-term memory. If you tell him a phone number and ask him to repeat it, he will; but if you change the subject and then ask him the number, he can't remember. M.P. is going to be living in the present for the rest of his life. He has lost the essential ability of the self to evolve."

M.P. is uncannily similar to one of the most remarkable and intensively studied patients of all time, a man called H.M., who lost his memory after undergoing brain surgery to treat epilepsy. This type of memory loss, called anterograde amnesia, stops time. It usually results from damage to the hippocampus, which normally processes, discards, or dispatches information by sending signals to other parts of the brain.

"The hippocampus is critical for learning," says Gluck, "and it's also one of the most volatile, unstable parts of the brain—one of the first parts damaged if oxygen is cut off. Think of it as a highly maneuverable kayak; it has to immediately capture a whole range of information about an event and needs the ability to go rapidly through many changes. We think the hippocampus serves as a filter, learning new associations and deciding what is important and what to ignore or compress. That's why it's critical for learning." The hippocampus is, in a sense, a collating machine, sorting and then sending various packets of information to other parts of the brain.

One of the most exciting advances in neuroscience may lie ahead as researchers begin to actually model the living brain on the computer—creating a new era of artificial intelligence called neural networks. Gluck and researchers at New York University have begun to model the hippocampus, creating "lesions" and watching what happens—in the hope that they can develop specialized tests that will identify Alzheimer's in its early stages, as well as develop machinery that can learn the way a brain does. Thus far their predictions about its role have been borne out—in fact, Gluck is developing applications for the military so that hippocampal-like computers can learn the early signals of engine malfunctions and sound the alarm long before a breakdown.

The hippocampus does not store memories permanently. It is a way station, though a supremely important one. Like a football player in the heat of the game, it passes the ball to other parts of the brain. This takes minutes, or maybe even hours, according to James McGaugh, Ph.D., of the University of California at Irvine. At that point, memories can still be lost. They need to be consolidated; the network of neurons responsible for a memory needs to be strengthened through repeated stimuli, until the memory exists independent of the hippocampus, a process known as long-term potentiation (LTP).

Once again, a word picture of this process is extremely crude. In actuality, Edelman points out, "the circuits of the brain look like no others we have seen before. The neurons have tree-like arbors that overlap in myriad ways. Their signaling is like the vast aggregate of interactive events in a jungle."

No one is certain how long it takes to fully consolidate a memory. Days? Weeks? Perhaps it takes even years until the linkages of networks are so deeply engraved that the memory becomes almost crystallized—easy to recall, detailed and clear. Individuals like M.P. seem to lose several years of memory just prior to hippocampal damage; so do Alzheimer's patients, who usually suffer hippocampal damage as their brains begin to malfunction, and who recall their childhood days with fine-etched clarity but find the present blurred.

A Magic Rhythm of Memory?

Just how and when do memories become permanent? Scientists now have direct evidence of what they have long suspected—that consolidation of memories, or LTP, takes place during sleep or during deeply relaxed states. It is then that brain waves slow to a rhythm known as "theta," and perhaps, according to McGaugh, the brain releases chemicals that enhance storage.

In an ingenious experiment reported in the journal *Science* last July, researchers planted electrodes in different cells in rats' hippocampi, and watched each cell fire as the animals explored different parts of a box. After returning to their cages, the rats slept. And during sleep the very same cells fired.

There seems to be a specific brain rhythm dedicated to LTP. "It's the magic rhythm of theta! The theta rhythm is the natural, indigenous rhythm of the hippocampus," exclaims neuroscientist Gary Lynch, Ph.D., of the University of California at Irvine. Lynch is known for his inspiring, if slightly mad, brilliance. His laboratory found that LTP is strongest when stimulation is delivered to the hippocampus in a frequency that corresponds to the slow rhythms of theta, of deep relaxation. Research by James McGaugh seems to confirm this: the more theta waves that appear in an animal's EEG (electroencephalogram), the more it remembers.

No wonder, then, that recent experiments show sleep improves memory in humans—and specifically, the sleep associated with dreaming, REM (rapid eye movement) sleep. In Canada, students who slept after cramming for an exam retained more information than those who pulled an all-nighter. In Israel, researchers

Avi Karni and Dov Sagi at the Weizmann Institute found that interrupting REM sleep 60 times in a night completely blocked learning; interrupting non-REM sleep just as often did not. These findings give scientific punch to "superlearning" methods like that of Bulgarian psychiatrist Georgi Lozanov, which utilizes deep relaxation through diaphragmatic breathing and music, combined with rhythmic bursts of information.

The Haunted Brain

What happens when memory goes awry? It seems that some memories are so deeply engraved in the brain that they haunt an individual as if he were a character in an Edgar Allen Poe story. How, asks Roger Pittman, M.D., coordinator of research and development at the Manchester (New Hampshire) Veterans Administration Medical Center and associate professor at Harvard Medical School, does the traumatic event "carve its canyons and basins of memory into the living brain?"

In any kind of emotionally arousing experience, the brain takes advantage of the fight-or-flight reaction, which floods cells with two powerful stress hormones, adrenaline and noradrenaline. "We believe that the brain takes advantage of the chemicals released during stress and powerful emotions," says James McGaugh, "to regulate the strength of storage of the memory." These stress hormones stimulate the heart to pump faster and the muscles to tense; they also act on neurons in the brain. A memory associated with emotionally charged information gets seared into the brain. We owe our very lives to this: a dangerous, threatening, or exciting event needs to be recalled well so that we may take precautions when meeting similar danger again.

Scientists are now beginning to understand just how emotional memory works and why it is so powerful. According to Joseph Ledoux, Ph.D., of the Center for Neural Science at New York University, the hormones associated with strong emotion stimulate the amygdala, an almond-shaped organ in the brain's cortex.

It's long been known that when rats are subjected to the sound of a tone and a shock, they soon learn to respond fearfully to the tone alone. The shocker is that when the auditory cortex—the part of the brain that receives sound—is completely destroyed, the rats are still able to learn the exact same fear response. How can a rat learn to be afraid of a sound it cannot hear?

The tone, it appears, is carried directly back to the amygdala, as well as to the auditory cortex. Destroy the amygdala, and even a rat with perfect hearing will never learn to be afraid of the sound. As neurologist Richard Restak, M.D., notes, this "implies that much of our brain's emotional processing occurs unconsciously. The amygdala may process many of our unconscious fear responses." This explains in part why phobias are so difficult to treat by psychotherapy. The brain's memory for emotional experiences is an enduring one.

But the ability of the brain to utilize stress hormones can go badly awry—and a memory can become not simply permanent but intrusive and relentless. "Suppose somebody shoots you and years later you're still waking up in a cold sweat with nightmares," says McGaugh. "The hormonal regulation of memory, when pushed to an extreme in a traumatic situation, may make memories virtually indelible."

Such memories seem so powerful that even an innocuous stimulus can arouse them. Roger Pittman compares the inescapable memories of PTSD, where flashbacks to a nightmarish trauma intrude relentlessly on daily life, to a black hole, "a place in space-time that has such high gravity that even light cannot pass by without being drawn into it."

So with ordinary associations and memories in PTSD: "As all roads lead to Rome, all the patient's thoughts lead to the trauma. A war veteran can't look at his wife's nude body without recalling with revulsion the naked bodies he saw in a burial pit in Vietnam, can't stand the sight of children's dolls because their eyes remind him of the staring eyes of the war dead."

The tragic twist is that, Pittman believes, each time a memory floods in again, the same stress hormones are released, running the same neural paths of that particular memory and binding the victim ever tighter in the noose of the past. Yet in response to the stress of recalling trauma, the body releases a flood of calming opiates. These neurochemicals, which help us meet the immediate demands of stress and trauma, might create a kind of unfortunate biochemical reward for the traumatic memory. "This whole question of an appetitive component to trauma is really fascinating and as yet unexplored," notes Pittman. "It may explain the intrusive, repeating nature of these memories. Maybe, however horrible the trauma, there's something rewarding in the brain chemicals released."

A solution, then, to treating the kind of PTSD we see in war veterans and victims of rape and child abuse, might lie in blocking the action of some of these stress hormones. And perhaps a key to enhancing ordinary learning is to create a judicious amount of stress—excitement, surprise, even a healthy dose of fear (like the kind one may feel before cramming for a demanding final exam).

A landmark study recently reported by James McGaugh and Larry Cahill, in *Nature,* indicates that any emotion, even ordinary emotion, is linked to learning. They gave two groups of college students a drug that blocks the effects of adrenaline and noradrenaline, then showed the students a series of 12 slides that depicted scenes such as a boy crossing the street with his mother or visiting a man at a hospital. A control group was told an ordinary story (son and mother visit the boy's surgeon father) that corresponded to some of the slides. The experimental group heard a story of disaster (boy is hit by car; a surgeon attempts to reattach his severed feet).

Two weeks later, the volunteers were given a surprise memory test. Students who heard the ordinary story recalled all 12 slides poorly. The second group, however, recalled significantly better the slides associated with the story of disaster.

Then, in an ingenious twist, McGaugh and Cahill repeated the experiment with new volunteers. Just before the slide show, the experimental group was given a beta blocker—a drug that acts on nerve cells to block the effect of stress hormones. Two weeks later they could not be distinguished from the control group. They similarly remembered all 12 slides poorly.

The implications of this elegant experiment are far reaching. "Let's suppose," postulates McGaugh, "that a plane crashes near Pittsburgh and you're hired to pick out the body parts. If we give you a beta blocker, we impair your 'emotional' memory, the memory for the trauma, without impairing your normal memory."

Pittman looks forward in the next decade to drugs that not only block PTSD but help ameliorate it. "There seems to be a window of opportunity, up to six hours or so in rats in any case, before memories are consolidated." During that time effective drugs, such as beta blockers, might be administered.

Memory Lost and Regained

The stories are legendary. Elizabeth Loftus has found ordinary memory to be so malleable that she can prompt volunteers to "remember nonexistent broken glass and tape recorders; to think of a clean-shaven man as having a mustache, of straight hair as curly, of hammers as screwdrivers, to place a barn in a bucolic scene that contained no buildings at all, to believe in characters who never existed and events that never happened."

Sometimes the memories become so seemingly fantastical that they lead to court cases and ruined lives. "I testified in a case recently in a small town in the state of Washington," Loftus recalls, "where the memories went from, 'Daddy made me play with his penis in the shower' to 'Daddy made me stick my fist up the anus of a horse,' and they were bringing in a veterinarian to talk about just what a horse would do in that circumstance. The father is ill and will be spending close to $100,000 to defend himself."

Nobody is quite sure how memories might be lost to us and then later retrieved—so-called repression. Whatever it is, it is a different process than traumatic amnesia, a well-known phenomenon where a particular horrendous event is forgotten because it was never consolidated in long-term memory in the first place. Such is the amnesia of an accident victim who loses consciousness after injury. Repressed memory, on the other hand, is alleged to involve repeated traumas.

According to UCLA's Daniel Siegel, both amnesia and repression may be due to a malfunction of the hippocampus. In order to recall an explicit memory, and to be able to depict it in words and pictures, the hippocampus must process it first. Perhaps, postulates Siegel, the work of the hippocampus is disrupted during trauma—while other components of memory carry on. We know, for example, that primitive responses like fear or excitement stimulate the amygdala directly; learning can occur without our "knowing" it.

If explicit memory is impaired—you forget what happened to you—but implicit memory is intact, you may still be profoundly influenced by an experience. Siegel thinks that some individuals remove conscious attention during repeated trauma, say from an unbearable event like repeated rapes. In the parlance of the mind trade, they "dissociate."

While his theory may explain repressed memory plausibly, it doesn't suggest how the memory emerges decades later, explicit and intrusive. And it doesn't answer the contention of many researchers that such repression is probably rare, and that the wave of repressed memories we are hearing about today may be due to invention.

It turns out that it's relatively easy to confuse imagery with perception. The work of Stephen Kossyln, Ph.D., a psychologist at Harvard University and author of *Image and Brain* (MIT press), has shown that the exact same centers in the brain are activated by both imagination and perception. "PET studies have shown that, when subjects close their eyes and form visual images, the same areas are activated as if they were actually seeing." The strength of the imagined "signal" (or image) is about half that of a real one. Other research shows that the source of a memory—the time, place, or way the memory began—is the first part to fade. After all, the source of a memory is fragile.

If we concentrate on generating images that then get recorded in the web of neurons as if they were real, we might actually convince ourselves that confabulations are true. (This might also explain how some individuals who lie about an event eventually convince themselves, through repeated lying, that the lie is true.)

The fragility of source memory explains why, in a famous experiment by psychologist John Neisser, John Dean's testimony about Richard Nixon was shown to be both incredibly accurate and hugely inaccurate. "His initial testimony was so impressive that people called him a human tape recorder," recalls psychologist Charles Thompson, Ph.D. "Neisser then compared the actual tapes to his testimony, and found that if you really looked at the specifics, who said what and when, Dean was wrong all over the place. But if you just looked at his general sense of what was going on in the meetings he was right on target. His confusion was about the source." In general, supposes Thompson, this is how memory works. We have an accurate sense of the core truth of an event, but we can easily get the details wrong.

"Memory is more reconstructive than reproductive. As time passes, details are lost. We did a study where we asked people to keep a daily diary for up to a year and a half, and later asked them questions about recorded events. The memory of the core event and its content stayed at a high level of about 70 percent, while the peripheral details dropped quickly."

Can Memory Create the Self?

From Freud on down, it was believed that memories from infancy or early childhood were repressed and somehow inaccessible—but that their clues, like the bits of bread dropped by Hansel and Gretel in the forest, could be found in dreams or in the pathology of waking life. Now we know better. It's that the brain systems that support declarative memory develop late—two or three years into life.

If we don't actually lay down any memories of our first few years, how can they shape our later life? An intriguing answer can be pieced together from findings from far-flung researchers.

Daniel Siegel plows the field of childhood memory and attachment theory. He finds that memory is profoundly affected in children whose mothers had rejected or avoided them. "We don't know why this happens, but at 10 years old, these children have a unique paucity in the content of their spontaneous autobiographical narratives." As adults, they do not recall childhood family experiences.

It may be that memory storage is impaired in the case of childhood trauma. Or it may be, Siegel suggests, that avoidant parents don't "talk to children about their experiences and memories. Those children don't have much practice in autobiographical narrative. Not only are their memories weak or nonexistent, the sense of self is not as rich. As a psychotherapist, I try to teach people to tell stories about their lives. It helps them develop a richer sense of self."

As far as the biology of the brain goes, this may be no different than training an 18-year-old boy to distinguish between whales and submarines; if the hippocampus is continually fed a stimulus, it will allocate more of the brain's capacities to recording and recognizing that stimulus. In the case of autobiographical narrative, however, what emerges is magical and necessary: the self.

That is almost like saying memory creates the self, and in a sense it does. But memory is also created and recreated by the self. The synergy between the two is like two sticks rubbed together in a forest, creating fire. "We now have a new paradigm of memory," notes Loftus, "where memories are understood as creative blendings of fact and fiction, where images are alchemized by experience and emotion into memories."

"I think it's safe to say we make meaning out of life, and the meaning-making process is shaped by who we are as self," says Siegel. Yet that self is shaped by the nature of memory. "It's this endless feedback loop which maintains itself and allows us to come alive."

When we think of our lives, we become storytellers—heroes of our own narrative, a tale that illumines that precious and mysterious "self" at the center. That "I am" cannot be quantified or conveyed precisely and yet it feels absolute. As Christopher Isherwood wrote long ago in *The Berlin Stories,* "I am a camera." Yet, as the science is showing us, there is no single camera—or if there is, it is more like the impressionist, constantly shifting camera of *Last Year at Marienbad.* Memory is malleable—and so are we.

❦❦❦

Name ______________________________ Date ______________ Period ________

Chapter 8

It's Magical! It's Malleable! It's . . . Memory

1. Who is Elizabeth Loftus and why is she important to this article?

2. Why has the issue of repressed memory, which should be a psychological debate, been of interest to lawmakers?

3. Why does the author claim that memory must occasionally make errors?

4. What organ in the brain is the center, or hub, or memory? What does it do?

Name ______________________ Date ______________ Period ________

Chapter 8

It's Magical! It's Malleable! It's . . . Memory

5. How do scientists explain the fact that "flight-or-fight" experiences become very strong memories?

____

____

____

____

____

6. Discuss what you think researcher Charles Thompson meant by his statement "Memory is more reconstructive than reproductive."

____

____

____

____

____

7. Write a paragraph about what life would be like without the ability to form long-term memories.

____

____

____

____

____

____

____

How To Make a Better Student: Seven Kinds of Smart

James Collins

This article first appeared in Time Magazine on October 19, 1998. James Collins interviewed Howard Gardner on his theory of multiple intelligences.

Did you know that you are smart in all sorts of different ways?"

Niki Mitchell is addressing her class of kindergartners on one of their first days at Coyote Creek Elementary School in Highland Ranch, Colo., a spanking-new middle-class suburb of Denver. A dozen neatly dressed five-year-olds sit on the floor in front of Mitchell as she points to a chart on the wall that lists different kinds of "smart." She describes each of them. "Maybe you like to draw pictures. That means you're picture-smart," she offers, then explains what it means to be word-smart, number-smart, body-smart, people-smart and music-smart . . . "We're lots of these smarts," she says.

The children in Mitchell's class are among the newest initiates of the philosophy that is probably exciting more educators than any other right now. Like many schools around the country, Coyote Creek has based its instruction on Howard Gardner's theory of multiple intelligences, or MI. Gardner, a professor at the Harvard Graduate School of Education, first proposed the theory in his book Frames of Mind, which was published in 1983. Since then, Gardner's ideas have received widespread attention and acceptance among parents and have been eagerly embraced by teachers. "Multiple intelligences is clearly the biggest thing right now," says Jim Bellanca, president of a teacher-training company called SkyLight Publishing and Training. Bellanca says that since 1992, SkyLight has provided training in MI to some 30,000 teachers and school administrators.

The increasing use of MI in schools raises a very simple question: Is this a good thing? The answer is not so simple, but there are good reasons to have doubts about this trend. To be sure, cognitive psychologists and educational researchers tend to give Gardner high praise for helping the public understand that intelligence is multifaceted, and MI has undoubtedly helped teachers understand and value the various talents a child has. Nevertheless, evidence for the specifics of Gardner theory is weak, and there is no firm research showing that its practical applications have been effective. No one says that using MI in schools is directly injurious. The danger is that it leads to wasted time, to an emphasis on less important skills and to a false sense that learning has taken place when it has not.

Sitting in his spare office at Harvard on a recent morning, a small dugout canoe made by his son resting on a nearby table, Howard Gardner talked about his work and the use others have made of it. A slender man with a soft face and hair flopping over his forehead, Gardner looks a bit like the concert pianist he might have been if he had pursued that career. After a long discussion of the merits of his theory, he tried to sum up his views. "Here's a credo I've never stated before," he said. "I'm sure there are lots of different intelligences. I'm sure kids differ in their profiles. I'm sure an educational approach that pays attention to this is going to be more effective than one that denies it."

Expressed at this level of generality, Gardner's theory is one with which few people could disagree. But the purpose of Frames of Mind was to identify seven specific "intelligences," and that list forms the basis of all the educational applications of MI. Gardner argued against the view of intelligence as a single faculty that is accurately measured by an IQ test. Rather, he said, we have several separate intellectual capacities, each of which deserves to be called an intelligence. The seven intelligences are linguistic, musical, logical-mathematical, spatial, bodily-kinesthetic, interpersonal (the ability to understand others) and intrapersonal (the ability to understand oneself). More recently, Gardner has added a "naturalist" intelligence.

Gardner based his list on findings from neurology, developmental and cognitive psychology, and anthropology. He argued that these intelligences can be shown to be localized in the brain; that they are exhibited in extreme form by idiots savants, prodigies and geniuses; that they have a clear developmental history; and that they are used in the performance of roles that cultures value around the world. In the book's final section, Gardner explored the educational implications of the theory, suggesting ways the intelligences can be exploited and fostered.

Those who hold that intelligence is a single, general ability and those who say it consists of many factors have engaged in a long-standing, bitter debate (although even those who believe in general intelligence say there are many subordinate cognitive abilities). Reviewers praised Frames of Mind for eloquently making new arguments on behalf of the multifaceted position, but they complained that Gardner's theory is too speculative. "The discussion is all hunch and opinion," wrote George Miller, one of the founders of cognitive psychology. The eminent developmental psychologist Jerome Bruner, a onetime colleague of Gardner's, said the book was "in many ways brilliant" but that Gardner succeeded "only moderately well" in proving the existence and independence of the seven intelligences. In particular, Bruner said, the arguments for the kinesthetic and personal intelligences "stumble badly."

Some of the strongest doubts about Gardner's evidence were expressed in Frames of Mind by Gardner himself. "The most I can hope to accomplish here is to provide a feeling for each specific intelligence," he wrote. "I am painfully aware that a convincing case for each candidate intelligence remains the task of other days and other volumes." And at the very end of the book, he warned that his work "needs to be amply discussed and tested" in the fields of biology and cognitive science before it is put into practice. "We are not yet certain," he said, "of the goodness of the idea of multiple intelligences."

In the 15 years since Frames of Mind was published, those other volumes have never appeared. Nor, as Gardner acknowledges, have those discussions and tests been undertaken. He now says that as a scientist he preferred to move on to other matters within MI and outside it. Moreover, he says, it goes against the grain of his philosophy to develop tests to measure the intelligences, a prerequisite psychologists say would be necessary to determine the validity of the theory. Gardner also points out that the overall trends in neurology and cognitive psychology strongly support his view that intelligence comprises many abilities.

Gardner is right about that. Still, many neurologists and psychologists believe recent discoveries in brain science—the localization of particular traits, the proliferation and pruning of synapses—are far too poorly understood to guide educators. Meanwhile, students of cognition, even those who give Gardner much credit, cite research that contradicts him. "The different intelligences show correlations in many cases, and within intelligence, there is a lack of unity," said Robert Sternberg, a professor of psychology and education at Yale. In other words, some of Gardner's intelligences do not seem to be independent faculties, while other intelligences divide up into more than one faculty.

As science, then, there may be less to the theory of multiple intelligences than many educators seem to believe. That may not matter so much. Gardner and other researchers say it's not necessary for a theory to enjoy absolute scientific confirmation as long as it shows good results in the classroom. But does MI show such results?

Gardner has never laid down a detailed plan for applying his theory in schools, and the consultants and publishers who offer training in MI operate independently of him, so there is a wide range of actual practices. A few hundred schools, like Coyote Creek, use the theory in a thoroughgoing way; thousands more adopt pieces of it. The result is that the methods that go under the name of multiple intelligences are often ones Gardner would not approve of. He insists, for example, that it is a waste of time to simply "exercise the intelligence muscles."

Yet the most common use of MI is to attack a topic from seven directions to fit in all the intelligences. Take a typical project described in a book published by SkyLight. To teach children about the oceans, it is suggested that they write about cleaning a fish (tapping the linguistic intelligence), draw a sea creature (spatial), "role play" a sea creature (bodily-kinesthetic), use a Venn diagram to compare and contrast ships (logical), tap glasses with different amounts of water (musical), design a water vehicle in a group (interpersonal) and choose a favorite sea creature (intrapersonal). All these activities will take up a lot of time, and they will teach children very little about the ocean.

The key for Gardner is first to decide on the facts and procedures a teacher wants a student to understand, and then to figure out how best to present this information, given the student's strengths and weaknesses. Jean McKibben, a fifth-grade teacher at Coyote Creek, provided an example of such an approach when she described a project her students did about the European settlement of the Americas. Among other things, she wanted them to learn about the boats that were used.

"Dave has a lot of trouble getting things down on paper," McKibben said of one pupil. "His main emphasis is doing things with his hands. His model of the boat was fantastic. It showed he really knew the information. If I asked him to write it down, it would have been very short." This is just the kind of application Gardner envisions: because McKibben knew that Dave understood the world in a kinesthetic way, she was better able to teach him and assess his knowledge. Dave must still learn to write well, McKibben said, but what counted here was that he showed good understanding of the material.

Yet it is possible to raise objections even to an exemplary use of Gardner's theory. Is it a better use of Dave's time to work on his writing or to express himself kinesthetically? Gardner has claimed that "all the intelligences have equal claim to priority," but historically, verbal and math skills may be stronger predictors of job performance than he allows, and employers seem to be placing a higher and higher premium on them. Then there is the problem of superficiality. How deeply can a student comprehend a given topic by relying on his strongest intelligence? Using his hands, Dave may be able to learn about the boats of the settlers, but can a kinesthetic approach help him understand central historical issues, like the reasons the Europeans came to America in the first place?

A new article by Gardner, which he regards as quite important, suggests that the problem of depth remains to be solved. In "Multiple Approaches to Understanding" (to appear next year in an anthology), he sets out to show how MI theory can be used to teach evolution and the Holocaust. He first details inviting "entry points" for these topics—students strong in interpersonal intelligence, for example, could play the roles of different species. An entry point is only that, however, and Gardner proceeds to pose the "crucial educational question": Can we use knowledge about individual strengths to convey the "core notions" of a subject? One expects Gardner to answer this question, using illustrations from his two topics. Instead, he goes off into generalities. The reader is left with no idea of how Gardner would, say, use students' interpersonal gifts to teach them the core mathematical principles of genetics.

In 1993 Gardner published Multiple Intelligences: The Theory in Practice, a collection of articles written with colleagues at Harvard. The book is quite diffuse and unsystematic, and the samples in the projects described are very small. When TIME asked Gardner what evidence there was that MI has improved achievement in schools, there was a long pause before he answered, "The testimonials and figures are numerous enough from lots of different places to suggest it's worth taking seriously." (One such testimonial could come from Coyote Creek, which scores above the district average on standardized tests.) Gardner was saying there is plenty of anecdotal evidence in support of MI but no formal studies. This is not an irredeemable flaw, and others agree with Gardner that MI merits further investigation. "The ideas," says Robert Siegler of Carnegie Mellon University, "have enough support that it would be worthwhile implementing them on a large enough scale to find out if they work." At the moment, however, we don't know that they work.

When evaluating the use of Gardner's theory in schools, it is easy for people to let their emotions run away with them. The notion that a child may have important abilities that are not measured by IQ tests is immensely appealing; it also happens to be true. As Siegler said, "Howard sells hope." Yet this hope ought to be tempered by realism, and a realistic view of MI theory may not justify the enthusiasm it has engendered thus far.

❦❦❦

Name ______________________________ Date ______________ Period ________

Chapter 9

How To Make a Better Student: Seven Kinds of Smart

1. What question about the theory of multiple intelligence does the author explore? In other words, what is the basis for the article and what does Collins want the reader to decide?

____

____

____

____

____

____

2. What is the main criticism of Gardner's theory by psychologists such as Miller and Bruner, and how does Gardner answer this charge?

____

____

____

____

____

____

3. The author believes many schools are not applying Gardner's theory as he himself would, and gives an example using the ocean. What point was the author making?

____

____

____

____

____

Name ______________________ Date ______________ Period ________

Chapter 9

How To Make a Better Student: Seven Kinds of Smart

4. What does Siegler mean when he says at the end of the article that "Howard sells hope"?

5. What application, if any, does Gardner's theory have for employers? Do you think employers would change procedures to appeal to varying learning styles?

6. What do you think is your strongest intelligence?

Jean Piaget, Childhood Secrets

Seymour Papert

MIT professor Seymour Papert (inventor of the Logo computer language) worked with child psychologist Jean Piaget in Geneva, Switzerland. Papert wrote this article for Time Magazines "100 important people of the 20th century" series—this particular group of 100 looked at scientists.

Jean Piaget, the pioneering Swiss philosopher and psychologist, spent much of his professional life listening to children, watching children and poring over reports of researchers around the world who were doing the same. He found, to put it most succinctly, that children don't think like grownups. After thousands of interactions with young people often barely old enough to talk, Piaget began to suspect that behind their cute and seemingly illogical utterances were thought processes that had their own kind of order and their own special logic. Einstein called it a discovery "so simple that only a genius could have thought of it."

Piaget's insight opened a new window into the inner workings of the mind. By the end of a wide-ranging and remarkably prolific research career that spanned nearly 75 years—from his first scientific publication at age 10 to work still in progress when he died at 84—Piaget had developed several new fields of science: developmental psychology, cognitive theory and what came to be called genetic epistemology. Although not an educational reformer, he championed a way of thinking about children that provided the foundation for today's education-reform movements. It was a shift comparable to the displacement of stories of "noble savages" and "cannibals" by modern anthropology. One might say that Piaget was the first to take children's thinking seriously.

Others who shared this respect for children—John Dewey in the U.S., Maria Montessori in Italy and Paulo Freire in Brazil—fought harder for immediate change in the schools, but Piaget's influence on education is deeper and more pervasive. He has been revered by generations of teachers inspired by the belief that children are not empty vessels to be filled with knowledge (as traditional pedagogical theory had it) but active builders of knowledge—little scientists who are constantly creating and testing their own theories of the world. And though he may not be as famous as Sigmund Freud or even B. F. Skinner, his contribution to psychology may be longer lasting. As computers and the Internet give children greater autonomy to explore ever larger digital worlds, the ideas he pioneered become ever more relevant.

Piaget grew up near Lake Neuchatel in a quiet region of French Switzerland known for its wines and watches. His father was a professor of medieval studies and his mother a strict Calvinist. He was a child prodigy who soon became interested in the scientific study of nature. When, at age 10, his observations led to questions that could be answered only by access to the university library, Piaget wrote and published a short note on the sighting of an albino sparrow in the hope that this would influence the librarian to stop treating him like a child. It worked. Piaget was launched on a path that would lead to his doctorate in zoology and a lifelong conviction that the way to understand anything is to understand how it evolves.

After World War I, Piaget became interested in psychoanalysis. He moved to Zurich, where he attended Carl Jung's lectures, and then to Paris to study logic and abnormal psychology. Working with Theodore Simon in Alfred Binet's child-psychology lab, he noticed that Parisian children of the same age made similar errors on true-false intelligence tests. Fascinated by their reasoning processes, he began to suspect that the key to human knowledge might be discovered by observing how the child's mind develops.

Back in Switzerland, the young scientist began watching children play, scrupulously recording their words and actions as their minds raced to find reasons for why things are the way they are. In one of his most famous experiments, Piaget asked children, "What makes the wind?" A typical Piaget dialogue:

> *Piaget:* What makes the wind?
> *Julia:* The trees.
> *Piaget:* How do you know?
> *Julia:* I saw them waving their arms.
> *Piaget:* How does that make the wind?
> *Julia:* (waving her hand in front of his face): Like this. Only they are bigger. And there are lots of trees.
> *Piaget:* What makes the wind on the ocean?
> *Julia:* It blows there from the land. No. It's the waves . . .

Piaget recognized that five-year-old Julia's beliefs, while not correct by any adult criterion, are not "incorrect" either. They are entirely sensible and coherent within the framework of the child's way of knowing. Classifying them as "true" or "false" misses the point and shows a lack of respect for the child. What Piaget was after was a theory that could find in the wind dialogue coherence, ingenuity and the practice of a kind of explanatory principle (in this case by referring to body actions) that stands young children in very good stead when they don't know enough or have enough skill to handle the kind of explanation that grownups prefer.

Piaget was not an educator and never enunciated rules about how to intervene in such situations. But his work strongly suggests that the automatic reaction of putting the child right may well be abusive. Practicing the art of making theories may be more valuable for children than achieving meteorological orthodoxy; and if their theories are always greeted by "Nice try, but this is how it really is . . ." they might give up after a while on making theories. As Piaget put it, "Children have real understanding only of that which they invent themselves, and each time that we try to teach them something too quickly, we keep them from reinventing it themselves."

Disciples of Piaget have a tolerance for—indeed a fascination with—children's primitive laws of physics: that things disappear when they are out of sight; that the moon and the sun follow you around; that big things float and small things sink. Einstein was especially intrigued by Piaget's finding that seven-year-olds insist that going faster can take more time—perhaps because Einstein's own theories of relativity ran so contrary to common sense.

Although every teacher in training memorizes Piaget's four stages of childhood development (sensorimotor, preoperational, concrete operational, formal operational), the better part of Piaget's work is less well known, perhaps because schools of education regard it as "too deep" for teachers. Piaget never thought of himself as a child psychologist. His real interest was epistemology—the theory of knowledge—which, like physics, was considered a branch of philosophy until Piaget came along and made it a science.

Piaget explored a kind of epistemological relativism in which multiple ways of knowing are acknowledged and examined nonjudgmentally, yet with a philosopher's analytic rigor. Since Piaget, the territory has been widely colonized by those who write about women's ways of knowing, Afrocentric ways of knowing, even the computer's ways of knowing. Indeed, artificial intelligence and the information-processing model of the mind owe more to Piaget than its proponents may realize.

The core of Piaget is his belief that looking carefully at how knowledge develops in children will elucidate the nature of knowledge in general. Whether this has in fact led to deeper understanding remains, like everything about Piaget, controversial. In the past decade Piaget has been vigorously challenged by the current fashion of viewing knowledge as an intrinsic property of the brain. Ingenious experiments have demonstrated that newborn infants already have some of the knowledge that Piaget believed children constructed. But for those, like me, who still see Piaget as the giant in the field of cognitive theory, the difference between what the baby brings and what the adult has is so immense that the new discoveries do not significantly reduce the gap but only increase the mystery.

❦❦❦

Name ______________________ Date ______________ Period ________

Chapter 10

Jean Piaget, Childhood Secrets

1. What was the discovery made by Piaget that Albert Einstein said was "so simple that only a genius could have thought of it"?

____

____

____

____

____

____

2. Why has Piaget been thought of as an educational reformer, such as Dewey or Montessori, when he did not study schools or curriculum?

____

____

____

____

____

____

3. Why did Piaget believe it was unwise to continually correct children's explanation of events, even if they were wrong by adult standards?

____

____

____

____

____

Name ______________________________ Date ______________ Period ________

Chapter 10

Jean Piaget, Childhood Secrets

4. What is epistemology?

____

____

____

____

____

____

____

____

5. Think back to a time when you remember hearing (or even giving!) an explanation for an event that was not scientifically accurate, but that seemed logical and believable. Describe the event and the explanation.

____

____

____

____

____

____

____

____

____

____

____

Chapter 11 Adolescence

Adolescent Friends Not Always a Bad Influence

Hugh McIntosh

This article first appeared in the APA Monitor. The Monitor is the official periodical of the American Psychological Association.

Early last year, a 14-year old boy and his best friend planned and committed the murder of the boy's mother in a small Minnesota town.

Would the boy have killed his mother on his own? Perhaps not, suggests Willard Hartup, PhD, a University of Minnesota psychologist who studies peer relations in adulthood and early adolescence: "This murder was an unlikely event until these two antisocial friends reached consensus about it."

Only in the last decade have psychologists begun to explore the effects friendships have on adolescent development, the processes by which teens form friendships and the factors that influence their relationships.

Research has led to some surprising findings: teen "crowds" often ease the transition through adolescence, teens usually encourage each other in positive rather than negative ways and that parents may have far more sway with their adolescents than they realize.

Choosing Friends

Psychologists have long recognized that teen-agers make friends with people who are similar to themselves. New research finds that teen cultures or crowds facilitate friend selection. According to psychologist Bradford Brown, PhD, of the University of Wisconsin at Madison, crowds of "jocks," "druggies," "populars," "brains," "nerds" and "normals" channel adolescents toward particular relationships with peers.

"When kids choose a particular dress and grooming style, a set of activities on weekends, they're more or less placing themselves in a particular niche within the adolescent-peer social world that limits the kinds of relationships they're going to have with peers," Brown said.

Crowds engage adolescents at a time when they seek conformity. More important, these groups help teens develop identity and regulate social interactions.

Brown and his colleagues have also found that small groups of close friends wield more influence with adolescents than individual friends. In studies of adolescent peer groups of four or five, they found that clique characteristics predicted behavioral change in teens better than the qualities of the closest friend.

Influences of Peers

Peer influence can be positive or negative, but it's more likely to be the former than the latter, says psychologist Thomas Berndt, PhD, of Purdue University, who studies adolescent friendships and friends' influence.

Researchers have found, for example, that teens who did not smoke cigarettes reported their friends discouraged smoking, whereas children who smoked had friends whom they perceived as tolerating, rather than encouraging, smoking.

Berndt's own research on academic achievement showed that teens report their friends encourage them to do well in school instead of telling them not to worry about doing well.

But peer influence can be negative as well. As in the case of the mother's murder, teens are vulnerable to a "contagion effect," Berndt says. The theory holds that people in highly cohesive groups sometimes do things that they wouldn't do alone.

"The simple fact that the friend is there, even if the friend is not different in his attitudes from yours, makes antisocial acts more likely." Berndt said.

Research has also found that when deviant adolescents select deviant friends, their antisocial behaviors perpetuate in a downward spiral. In his studies of adolescents with high levels of alcohol and drug use, psychologist Michael Windle, PhD. of the Research Institute on Addiction in Buffalo, N.Y., found higher levels of arguments and other overt hostility among boys and more gossiping, rumor spreading and other covert hostility among girls than in teen friendships not involving deviant behavior.

In a year-long study of friendships among deviant adolescents, Windle found that alcohol and drug abuse and delinquency became worse over time. He also found, however, that teens involved in delinquent behavior practiced a high degree of self-disclosure with their peers. Even though their friendships were more hostile and less reciprocal than average, these adolescents were looking for someone to talk with about their problems.

"Unfortunately, if they're in a highly deviant peer network, they're not likely to get a lot of constructive ideas of what they should do about their situation," Windle said.

Influence of Parents

Although teens might not like it, parents can have an enormous influence on how they deal with friendships, experts say. An authoritative parenting style—which combines control and warmth—is particularly effective in moderating peer influence, says research psychologist Nina Mounts, PhD, of the University of Illinois at Urbana-Champaign. Authoritative parents exercise a high degree of control but negotiate many of the particulars, such as a curfew time.

In a study of ninth- through 11th-graders, Mounts and a colleague found that adolescents with authoritative parents were more strongly influenced by high-achieving friends and less influenced by drug-using friends than those with less authoritative parents. Mounts also found that some parents directly influence their adolescents' friendships through management techniques, such as inviting over pro-social friends or advising teen-agers not to hang out with certain friends. Her study found that teens whose parents used moderate amounts of management used drugs the least. Adolescents whose parents used higher or lower amounts had higher drug-use levels.

In addition, while friends influenced day-to-day issues, such as choice of clothes, parents influenced long-term issues such as educational choices.

It's difficult for parents to pick their teens' friends, said Brown. But they can help their children master the social skills needed for the new kinds of friendships formed at this age. And they can pick the environments from which their adolescents will select friends, if they have the foresight to nurture those environments in early childhood.

Name ______________________ Date ______________ Period ________

Chapter 11

Adolescent Friends Not Always a Bad Influence

1. What are the three "surprising" findings about the effects of adolescent friendships reported in this article?

____

____

____

____

____

____

2. Why do teens generally choose friends that are more like themselves than not?

____

____

____

____

____

____

3. Teens involved in deviant behavior often share a lot of information about themselves with their friends. Does this have a positive or negative effect, according to the author?

____

____

____

____

____

____

Name ______________________ Date ______________ Period ________

Chapter 11

Adolescent Friends Not Always a Bad Influence

4. According to the author, which parenting style is most effective in moderating peer influences?

5. Do you think your peer group has more positive or negative influences on you? Support your answer with specific examples.

Chapter 12 Adulthood and Aging

Brain Power

Joannie M. Schrof

Ms. Schrof is a free lance writer of psychology and other science-related articles, such as this one published in U.S. News and World Report.

Will old age destroy the mind? The prospect is so terrifying that the mind itself exiles the thought until those times when it cannot be ignored, such as the recent announcement that former President Ronald Reagan suffers from Alzheimer's disease. The fear is that even if one is lucky enough to escape Alzheimer's and other diseases that attack the brain, old age inevitably brings about the mind's decline. Indeed, an effigy of a feeble-minded old wretch lies deeply entrenched in the American psyche, leaving many to loathe the idea of growing old nearly as much as death itself. That spunky old aunt who's sharp as a tack provides little comfort, precisely because she seems such an outstanding exception. And short of a crystal ball, there has been no way of knowing if one will follow in her lively footsteps or end up unable to remember the names of beautiful grandchildren.

Myth #1: It Only Gets Worse. You are not inevitably destined for a steep mental decline. A third of those over 70 function as well as ever.

But now a group of scientists who study the aging brain are piecing together enough information to offer a hopeful judgment on the fate of our minds. While virtually no old brain matches the peak performance of its heyday, neither does it slide into a state of oblivion. From neuroscientists who study the brain in action to clinical psychologists who work with the elderly in their everyday lives, researchers are finding that severe mental decline is not inevitable and that an old brain has surprising abilities and strengths. One by one, they are debunking myths about what happens when the mind ages.

It Only Gets Worse

The notion that the mind naturally decays had been fostered by tests showing that the average 70-year-old takes longer and makes more mistakes than the typical 20-year-old on mental challenges ranging from memorizing lists to finding matching photos from a pile. But hidden within those results is the countervailing fact that, starting around the age of 50, people of similar ages begin to differ more and more from one another in their mental performance—some capacities drop noticeably, others remain steady or may actually rise. "You can safely draw general conclusions about the abilities—from athletic or cognitive skills—of a given 40-year-old," says Harvard University psychologist Douglas Powell. "But the only thing you can assume about a 65- or 75-year-old is how many candles will be on the birthday cake."

Powell's forthcoming book, *Profiles in Cognitive Aging,* describes a study showing that nearly a third of individuals enjoy steady lucidity throughout their twilight years. He tested 1,583 persons from 25 to 92 years of age in areas such as math and reading comprehension and found that on various tests, a quarter to a third of subjects in their 80s performed as well as younger counterparts. Even the lowest scorers suffered fairly modest declines that did not interfere with daily living. Perhaps most encouraging, a small fraction of subjects in their 80s and 90s—those Powell calls optimal agers—had exceptional scores that ranked them near the top of mental abilities for all ages.

Powell's findings mirror several other studies, including two major longitudinal studies conducted in Seattle and Baltimore over the past 35 years. They have traced more than 6,000 people and found that not only do most people retain strong mental skills until at least age 70 but over a fourth continue on well past that age without significant drops in brainpower. Yet another study found that a third of octogenarians performed on a par with the younger adults in such cognitive realms as making mental math calculations or remembering a string of random numbers.

Myth #2: Memory Is the First to Go. Your store of facts and procedures should be unaffected by age, but your capacity for abstract reasoning may fade over time.

Scientists suspect that many genetic and environmental factors play a part in distinguishing those who keep their faculties in prime shape from those who slide downhill (See "A Brain User's Guide to Aging"). K. Warner Schaie, a famed pioneer in the field of cognitive aging who designed the Seattle Longitudinal Study, finds that the factors most often associated with strong mental functions in older age groups include: an above-average level of education, a complex and stimulating lifestyle, and being married to a smart spouse. Factors such as a rigid adherence to routine and low satisfaction with life are associated with the earlier deterioration of the intellect. Yet, while researchers consistently find such correlations, they have yet to determine precisely how these things affect the aging brain.

Memory Is the First to Go

Perhaps the strongest belief about old age is that is causes forgetfulness. In scientific and popular literature, the idea has reigned for years that the aging brain's neurons die off by as many as 100,000 a year and with them the cherished memories of a lifetime. But, in fact, neurobiologists such as Gerald Fischbach at Harvard University have used modern cell-counting techniques to discover that, while many brain cells may shrink or grow dormant in old age, they do not die off in droves.

A look inside the living brain provides more assurance that the mind's storehouses of knowledge remain intact, though they may be tougher to tap into during old age. Neuroscientists who use the latest technology to view young and old brains at work find that it is primarily the brain's "hardware"—the billions of telephone-linelike connections and relay switches that act as processing equipment—that is vulnerable to wearing out with age. Meanwhile, the mind's "software"—the actual information that fills up the mind over a lifetime—does not deteriorate and, if anything, continues to grow more sophisticated with each passing year.

So, just as running the latest software program on an old computer will take more time and may involve glitches, one can possess a first-rate intelligence and still lose some speed and accuracy on cognitive challenges later in life. Debate continues over exactly when these trouble spots are likely to pop up. Some investigators say they can be detected as early as age 20; others say 40. Most agree that no mental decline occurs before 60 or 65 that affects a person's ability to function in the real world.

When mental abilities do pass their peak, memory is not the first to go, according to studies by Powell and others. Rather, it is usually the brain's capacity to make sense of spatial relationships—reading a map or finding your car when you exit a different door than you entered at the mall. Such difficulties often appear in the 40s. A decade later, the abstract reasoning required to make analogies dips downward. Following these, a type of memory known as "verbal memory after delay"—remembering details of a story after having turned attention to other tasks—starts to drop. But some mental skills, such as the ability to concentrate or do math calculations, seem to remain sturdy long into old age. And many studies find that certain types of memory—such as the "procedural" memory of how to play golf or ride a bicycle—are never touched by the aging process.

Even though some types of memory loss are common, they are not inevitable, according to pathbreaking work being done in an $8.4 million research consortium funded by the Charles A. Dana Foundation. Researchers in that project now believe that most types of memory loss should not be considered normal and could be treatable. For example, neurologists at Harvard are finding that the brain often ceases to produce a hormone involved in memory—acetylcholine—later in life. Tentative results suggest that psychoactive drugs could mimic the missing chemical and thereby reinvigorate the memory. At least a dozen other substances are also under investigation as potential memory boosters. "Saying you're going to lose your memory is like saying your car is going to break down," concludes Barry Gordon, director of the neurology division of the Johns Hopkins School of Medicine. "Sure, lots of cars do break down, but with the right maintenance and tuneups many never do."

Use It Or Lose It

Americans cherish the notion that exercising the mind will protect it from mental decay. But new research suggests a more nuanced aphorism: "Using it is good, but it doesn't guarantee that you won't lose it," says Denise Park, who directs the University of Georgia's Southeastern Center for Applied Cognitive Aging Research. There is no doubt that idle minds decay faster than those which are engaged in life, but scientists say there is not a straight connection between mental activity and mental acuity. For example, researchers have studied younger and older workers in dozens of professions and found that, from airline pilots to architects, the average older worker consistently performs worse on all sorts of basic cognitive ability tests than the younger worker. So much for not retiring.

Treating the brain to novel experiences and stimuli seems to be a key to keeping the mind agile. When Berkeley biologists Marian Diamond put old rats into cages with new toys, their brains exploded in activity, the neurons sprouting new connections that enlarged the blood flow to the brain enormously within days. But, even with several toys in the cage, this effect diminished before long as the novelty wore off and the rats became bored. And watching sports doesn't count as stimulation. When Diamond let rats passively observe other rats playing with toys, they didn't improve at all.

Myth #3: Use It Or Lose It. Yes, up to a point. But simply engaging in boring or repetitive mental activity won't stave off decline. Pursue eclectic interests.

Moreover, evidence suggests that it is not worth it to put the brain through mental workouts that aren't enjoyable. Powell found marked differences favoring older, highly active people who said they read widely in their spare time for pleasure over those who felt compelled to do so in order to "keep up." In other words: "Go ahead and do crossword puzzles if you enjoy them," says Cornell neuroscientist John P. Blass. But it probably won't help to force yourself through them if you hate them, he cautions. In fact, some studies find that the hard-driving types who insist on doing things as they've always been done are susceptible to declining more rapidly later in life. Conversely, Schaie, who is at Pennsylvania State University, identified the quality of mental flexibility—the willingness to improvise and to try unorthodox ways of doing things—as a prime predictor of mental vivacity in the later years.

Other research implies that emotional well-being may be just as influential on the aging mind as mental activity. Subjects who suffer frequently from negative emotions like depression, anxiety and anger tend to slide downhill more than those who find life satisfying. One biological explanation for this comes from Robert Sapolsky, author of *Stress, the Aging Brain, and the Mechanisms of Neuron Death.* He theorizes that the stress-related release of adrenal hormones bathes neurons in a dangerous chemical wash that can eventually damage the brain.

Sound Body, Sound Mind

It seems obvious that a sick body will sap one's mental powers, but in many cases illness does not devastate an aging brain. Eminent researcher Timothy Salthouse, author of *Theoretical Perspectives on Cognitive Aging,* reviewed numerous studies and concluded: "Contrary to intuition and popular opinion, there is little evidence that declines in cognitive performance are mediated by declines in health status." Rather, he finds, age-related drops are independent of both self-reported or objectively measured levels of health. Even those subjects who report themselves in the best physical condition don't differ from the group as a whole when it comes to test scores.

Myth #4: Sound Body, Sound Mind. Physical health does not always assist the vigor of your intellect; sometimes, exercise that's too intense may hurt your mental abilities.

Some diseases are linked to mental decline. Among them: heart disease, diabetes and high blood pressure. But Schaie and others have concluded that these diseases themselves probably do not cause the mental decline. Instead, they think that the overall lifestyles of patients might be to blame for both the physical and mental impairments. For instance: overeating, inactivity and stress show up as predictors for both physical and mental decay. Moreover, clinicians frequently find patients suffering from these illnesses who show no cognitive drops. Powell, for example, tested 50 retired Harvard professors in preparation for his larger study. "We found many people who checked the 'yes' box to all sorts of health problems, even heart attacks and strokes, then proceeded to perform like a dream on all the tests."

Exercise is a physical factor that seems most reliably to benefit the brainpower of the healthy and the sick, the young and old alike. But not all exercise is equal—those who engage in moderate exercise such as 30 minutes of walking a day score higher on tests than those who never exercise. But older people who spend hours a day running or swimming run some risks. Some studies show that scores begin to drop off again as the exercise level intensifies.

You Can't Teach An Old Dog New Tricks

Perhaps the best news from cognitive aging research is that even if you do lose it, you might be able to get it back again. An old brain retains an astonishing ability to rejuvenate itself. For example, Stanley Rapoport, chief of the neurosciences lab at the National Institute on Aging, compares the brains of younger and older people engaged in the same efforts and finds that older brains literally rewire themselves to compensate for losses. If one neuron isn't up to the job, neighboring brain cells help pick up the slack. As a result, Rapoport observes that as brains age they can actually shift responsibilities for a given task from one region to another.

This holds great promise for those seeking to help the elderly "relearn" skills and avoid the debilitating belief that they are irreversibly in decline. Schaie and his wife, Sherry Willis, also a Penn State researcher, found that subjects in their 70s who displayed marked losses in mental functioning over the past 14 years could greatly improve their performances through tutoring. After just five one-hour sessions aimed at bolstering basic abilities like reasoning and verbal skills and offering strategies for tackling tasks like memorization, some 40 percent regained everything they had lost over the years. Better yet, when researchers checked in on them seven years later, they still retained their elevated abilities. Likewise, Paul Baltes at the Max Planck Institute in Berlin trained elderly subjects to memorize an average string of 60 random numbers and 35 names, far more than most people in their prime could hope to do without training.

Myth #5: You Can't Teach An Old Dog New Tricks. An old brain can rewire itself to compensate for losses, and refresher courses can keep your mind sharp.

Clinical psychologists are using techniques not only to improve academic performance but also to keep the elderly sharp and independently functioning in their daily lives. In her University of Georgia lab, Park works with elderly subjects to lower the effort and anxiety attached to such common challenges as coordinating complicated medication regimens, remembering needed grocery items even if the list is lost and finding one's way around a new city.

No Myth: Older and Wiser

Not all cultures have looked upon the elderly as frail-minded. The Bible celebrates the wisdom of old King Solomon, and since ancient times Eastern cultures have revered their elders as gurus. One intriguing study conducted by Harvard's Ellen Langer and Rebecca Levy suggests that cultural norms may be self-fulfilling prophecies. In China, where age carries no connotation of stupor, the elderly perform much higher on tests than their American counterparts.

Scientists now have a way to measure "wisdom" and are confirming that it is an asset that grows with age. In Berlin, Baltes has developed a model defining wisdom as expertise in fundamental matters of life. One who meets Baltes's criteria for wisdom possesses such qualities as insight, sound judgment, perspective and the ability to weigh conflicting values and generate good problem-solving strategies. Researchers study wisdom in the lab by asking subjects to "think aloud" as they respond to life dilemmas, such as what to do when a friend calls threatening suicide or when a 15-year-old girl wants to get married. Not surprisingly, older people consistently outshine younger people on all measures of wisdom, offering more thoughtful, sophisticated advice. Not only do the older subjects prove more sagacious they also tend to score as high as publicly acclaimed "wise" figures in Germany and professionals, like social workers and therapists, trained to give advice about serious life problems.

In fact, many studies show that older people adjust to their slower-moving brains by simply being smarter and carrying out tasks more efficiently than younger counterparts. For example, one study found that older typists are able to match younger typists' speed by reading farther ahead in the text and by moving their fingers differently so as to conserve time and energy. Other research shows that, although it often takes older people longer than youngsters to make a decision, it is usually a better one.

There is now such a preponderance of evidence that older brains adjust cleverly to changing biology that leaders in the cognitive aging field describe older brains not as inferior, but simply as different from younger brains. Some researchers even say that in many ways, it is young people who are disadvantaged and compensate for a lack of crucial information, experience, expertise and wisdom with exceptionally speedy minds. Baltes posits that one day older folks may use their know-how to outwit biology and avoid decline altogether.

It is likely to take some time before researchers sort through the myriad factors that seem to aid or impede the aging mind. But never again will the scientific community define old age as a time of mental frailty. And in popular circles the ancient idea of the elder as sage is likely to find renewed vitality.

Name ______________________ Date ______________ Period ________

Chapter 12

Brain Power

1. Name three of the myths associated with cognitive aging.

2. What factors are associated with the early deterioration of the intellect?

3. What effect does exercise have on brain power?

Name ______________________________ Date ________________ Period __________

Chapter 12

Brain Power

4. What characteristics are associated with wisdom? How does it differ from intelligence?

5. What sort of behaviors can you adopt to decrease your likelihood of cognitive decline?

Gender Stereotypes and Roles

Susan A. Basow

Ms. Basow is the author of a recent textbook that examines how American sex-role stereotypes began; to what extent these images fit the majority of real people; how they are maintained and transmitted; how they affect females & males in our society; and how changes can be made.

Friendships

Female-Female Friendships Females as a group are more likely than males as a group to have close, intimate same-sex friendships. Female same-sex friendships have many positive qualities that are evident throughout the life span—trust, loyalty, enjoyment, nurturance, and attachment. Females converse with each other frequently and in great depth about such intimate topics as personal and family matters. Females tend to rate other females highly in terms of social support. Among feminist women and those who may be considered nonconventional (desirous of change and control over their lives, willing to take risks), same-sex friendships appear to be particularly important, close, and egalitarian, although the empirical data here are mixed. Overall, most women find their female friendships to be supportive and valuable. Indeed, some research suggests that the end of a friendship is more painful for a woman than the end of a romantic relationship, unlike the situation for men.

The establishment of close female friendships is facilitated by the socialization of females to value intimacy and connection. Girls grow up with a sense of self as embedded in relationships. A close relationship with one's mother correlates positively with intimacy in female friendships. Furthermore, the personality traits encouraged in females—sensitivity, empathy, nurturance, caring, expressiveness—facilitate the development of intimate relationships.

Still, although many aspects of the female role and stereotype facilitate female same-sex friendships, a number of obstacles to such relationships also exist. The general *taboo against displays of anger* in females makes it difficult for many girls to learn how to express and resolve angry feelings that inevitably arise in intimate relationships. Thus, girls may use covert rather than overt forms of aggression in their friendships. For example, the friendship patterns of young girls frequently alternate between inclusion and exclusion, intimacy and repudiation. Most girls either experience or observe a close relationship between "best friends" that is broken by a third girl, only to have the triad reassemble in a different configuration shortly thereafter. Despite the conflicts female friendships may involve, they are an important source of emotional support in times of personal crisis.

A second barrier to female same-sex friendships is *competition for males.* Since a female's identity traditionally has been determined by the status of the male to whom she is attached—for example, the high school football captain—girls may come to view other girls as competitors for the high-status males, thereby limiting friendships. Or they may view friendships with girls as unimportant, because no status accrues from such relationships. It is not uncommon for girls to break plans with their girlfriends if a date comes along. The girlfriend even is supposed to understand "the way it is."

Male-Male Friendships Despite the popular image of the closeness of male "buddies," in the past 15 years many male writers have acknowledged the poor quality of many male-male relationships. Although boys as a group do have some intimate friendships during adolescence, these friendships generally are concerned less with interpersonal intimacy and sensitivity than are those of girls. The "gang" serves as a source of support in case of conflict with adults, rather than as a source of emotional support in personal crises. For adolescent and young adult men, male bonding frequently occurs at the expense of other groups—whether those groups be other male gangs, gay men, or females. For example, the sexist joke telling and sexual harassment and assault against women that sometimes occur when males are together serve as ways for some males to feel close to each other and separate from females.

These gender differences in same-sex friendships appear to be due in part to gender differences in affiliation motivation and in part to different expectations regarding same-sex friendships. Females seem to expect more intimacy in their friendships than males, which continues throughout the life span. Furthermore, the meaning of intimacy appears to be different for males and females. For males, intimacy more often means doing things together or discussing work, sports, or politics. For females, intimacy more often means sharing feelings and concerns. Males tend to develop friendships with a wider network of other males to meet different needs, whereas females tend to develop a smaller network of other females to whom they can relate in a variety of areas. In other words, males tend to have separate "sports friends," "work friends," "drinking buddies," and so on, whereas females tend to have a single set of friends with whom they do everything.

The lack of emotional sharing in many male same-sex friendships means that many males do not receive maximum benefits from friendships—the relief of being able to release feelings with someone else and receive support, and the opportunity to broaden interests and perspective. In fact, many adult males never have had a close male friend or known what it means to share affection and concern with a male without fear of ridicule. As a result, men tend to report more feelings of loneliness than women, and the roots of their loneliness compared to that of women are more likely to lie in the lack of a cohesive set of friends.

As discussed earlier, being strong in expressive traits is most conducive to intimate relationships. Such traits generally are not encouraged in males. However, most males do appear capable of intimacy. For example, certain situational cues (like being asked to have an intimate conversation with their best friend) will elicit conversations similar to those that take place between female best friends. Thus, the lower level of intimacy in many male-male friendships seems to be due to a reluctance rather than an inability to be intimate. This reluctance to be intimate with another male probably stems from the male gender stereotype as inculcated through socialization practices—the emphasis on independence and competition, suppression of feelings and self-disclosure, an instilled fear of homosexuality, and the lack of appropriate role models.

Competitiveness is a major obstacle to male same-sex friendships. Most males are socialized early into believing that actions are more important than feelings and that they must compete in everything they do to "win" or come out on top. This intense male competition may pervade nearly every area of encounter among men, including sports, work, sex, and conversation. It makes intimate relationships among men most unlikely.

An even more important factor than competitiveness in inhibiting male friendships is the strong message most boys receive regarding *the need to suppress feelings*. Thus, maxims such as "Big boys don't cry," "Keep a stiff upper lip," and "Take it like a man" all pressure boys to keep their feelings hidden. If boys do not hide their emotions, they are likely to suffer marked loss in prestige, to be liked less, and to have difficulty assuming the competitive role society has set out for them. By sharing feelings, people become vulnerable. In a competitive atmosphere, this means that someone might take advantage of such vulnerability. According to male sex role prescriptions, showing feelings is weak and must be avoided at all costs.

Males begin to cover up their feelings as early as age 4. Yet the quality that most facilitates friendship formation is openness to others. Ironically, it is only in close relationships that men get emotional support, unlike the situation for women, who receive support from many different types of relationships, such as those among colleagues. Low self-disclosure in men explains why many male conversations tend to be monologues rather than give-and-take communications, since responding to another may reveal feelings. Another reason male conversations tend to be monologues may be that both of the men involved may try to dominate and interrupt the conversation.

Despite the barriers to intimate male-male friendships, men do appear to value the friendships they have. In most studies, males and females are equally satisfied with their same-sex friendships. Furthermore, although gender differences in friendship quality are consistent, the magnitude of the differences is not very large. In particular, most of the differences in friendship patterns have been found between sex-typed males and females. Few differences have been found in the same-sex friendships of androgynous females and males. Again, we must remember to be cautious about making extreme distinctions between the behavior of males and females in this and in other areas.

Male-Female Friendships If male-male friendships are difficult to establish, male-female ones are even more so. Most people have fewer other-sex friends than same-sex ones, although mixed-sex friendships have become more common among the younger generations. For example, in the mid-1980s, about one out of four college students named a member of the other sex as a best friend, whereas in the late 1970s, only 18% of a representative sample of middle-class Americans reported a close friendship with a member of the other sex.

Barriers Many barriers impede the establishment of cross-sex friendships, starting in preschool: gender segregation of activities, sexualization of male-female relationships, social pressures, ambiguity and lack of role models, sex-typed traits and behaviors, and gender inequality. All of these barriers are connected to gender stereotypes and gender roles.

Since to form friendships, people must first have an opportunity to get to know each other, the frequent *gender segregation of activities* inhibits the development of mixed-sex friendships. As we have seen, gender segregation begins during the pre-school years, is widespread, and continues to a large extent into adulthood. Such segregation allows the sexes to develop distinctive interaction styles, which exaggerate both perceived and actual gender differences. Both males and females tend to believe that members of the other sex are significantly different from themselves in attitudes, interests, and personal styles, even though actual gender differences in these areas are small and certainly are not found consistently. During college, both women and men think the other sex demands conformity to the gender stereotypes, even though such demands tend to be minimal. Both sexes also perceive other-sex peers as less trustworthy than same-sex peers, and these differences in perceptions of trust are apparent by the second grade. Since trust is critical in the formation of intimate relationships, cross-sex friendships are difficult to establish under these circumstances. Furthermore, in some cases, boys' early socialization to reject anything vaguely feminine may lead to fear and hatred of females. Such feelings are unlikely to facilitate friendship formation between the sexes.

Many people have difficulty believing that heterosexual males and females can have purely platonic relationships. Not only does this view add social pressure and external scrutiny to mixed-sex friendships that do not exist for same-sex friendships, this sexualized expectation affects participants in cross-sex friendships as well. That is, sexual feelings nearly always must be dealt with in mixed-sex friendships between heterosexual individuals, whereas their same-sex friendships typically don't bear this burden. Indeed, sexualized expectations make forming mixed-sex friendships extremely difficult. Many existing mixed-sex friendships are formed only after a sexual-romantic relationship has not worked out or when one party has clearly rejected the possibility of a sexual-romantic relationship. For these reasons, male-female relationships wherein one or both parties is homosexual are much less problematical than those wherein both parties are heterosexual. Because of the sexualization of male-female relationships, mixed-sex friendships are particularly difficult when one or both parties are married.

Gendered patterns of communication also make friendship formation between women and men difficult. In particular, since emotional sharing is the hallmark of an intimate relationship, males appear to be at a disadvantage in participating in such relationships. Indeed, some evidence exists that in mixed-sex relationships, females may provide a listening and support service ("ego boosting") for males without receiving any reciprocal service. It appears that both males and females prefer to self-disclose to another female, who may have had more experience and investment in being a good listener and in providing empathetic support. Thus, females may be less motivated than males by the prospect of obtaining needed emotional support in establishing a mixed-sex friendship.

Benefits Although the barriers just listed make the establishment of male-female friendships difficult, people who participate in such relationships generally find them to be rewarding. Mixed-sex friendships increase in frequency and intimacy during adolescence, with the transition occurring earlier for girls (seventh grade) than for boys (ninth grade).

We have noted that for males, females may be the only people to whom they can, or are willing to, self-disclose. Even (or especially) among married men, female friends remain important recipients of self-disclosures. It appears that females contribute emotional closeness and meaningfulness to an interaction, whether that interaction be with another female or male. In short, females make good friends. Not surprisingly, men are more likely than women to nominate a member of the other sex as a close friend and to look to other-sex rather than same-sex friendships for emotional intimacy and support. Furthermore, men tend to describe their cross-sex relationships as closer than do women. However, we must be careful about generalizing from research using mainly White participants to all males and females. Different sex-race groups appear to have different patterns of friendship.

In contrast to males, females rate their cross-sex friendships as less intimate and accepting than their same-sex friendships. Women see themselves as initiating more in cross-sex friendships and as wanting to give more than men. Women see more room for improvement in their cross-sex friendships than in their same-sex ones. If cross-sex friendships appear less rewarding than same-sex friendships for women, what motivates women to enter or maintain such mixed-sex relationships? Females receive a number of benefits from such friendships. In some situations, females feel more comfortable disclosing certain feelings (like love) to other-sex than to same-sex friends. Second, females often enjoy the companionship and the lesser intensity offered by male friends. Third, male friends, by virtue of their societal and gender status, also can offer status to their female friends. Furthermore, both sexes may enjoy the different perspectives offered by friends of the other sex. In particular, mixed-sex friendships allow each member to get an "insider's" view of how the other sex thinks.

In general, cross-sex friendships appear to involve more role playing and less spontaneity than same-sex friendships. Females are perceived as being dependent on the male friend, and males are perceived as being nurturant toward the female friend. Men tend to reveal mainly their strengths, and women their weaknesses, in cross-sex friendships. Despite these differences, mixed-sex friendships tend to be valued by those who have them. Such friendships may be a necessary step in breaking down the gender stereotypes, since, as social psychological research has established firmly, personal contact on an equal footing between members of disparate groups is necessary for the elimination of prejudice.

❦❦❦

Name ______________________ Date ______________ Period ________

Chapter 13

Gender Stereotypes and Roles

1. What two barriers to female same-sex friendships does the article discuss?

2. According to the article, what are the different meanings of intimacy for women and men?

3. What are the obstacles to male same-sex friendships?

Name ______________________________ Date ______________ Period ________

Chapter 13

Gender Stereotypes and Roles

4. In what ways do conventional gender roles have a positive effect on friendships?

5. What, in your experience, is the greatest barrier to same-sex friendships?

Chapter 14 Theories of Personality

How The Mind Works

Steven Pinker

How The Mind Works by MIT psychologist Steven Pinker is an informative survey of the modern brain. He shows us "where it came from, and how it lets us see, think, feel, interact, and pursue higher callings like art, religion, and philosophy." In this excerpt he looks at personality.

Personalities differ in at least five major ways: whether a person is sociable or retiring (extroversion-introversion), whether a person worries constantly or is calm and self-satisfied (neuroticism-stability), whether the person is courteous and trusting or rude and suspicious (agreeableness-antagonism), whether a person is careful or careless (conscientiousness-undirectedness), and whether a person is daring or conforming (openness-nonopenness). Where do these traits come from? If they are genetic, identical twins should share them, even if they were separated at birth, and biological siblings should share them more than adoptive siblings do. If they are a product of socialization by parents, adoptive siblings should share them, and twins and biological siblings should share them more when they grow up in the same home than when they grow up in different homes. Dozens of studies have tested these kinds of predictions on thousands of people in many countries. The studies have looked not only at these personality traits but at actual outcomes in life such as divorce and alcoholism. The results are clear and replicable, and they contain two shockers.

One result has become well known. Much of the variation in personality—about fifty percent—has genetic causes. Identical twins separated at birth are alike; biological siblings raised together are more alike than adopted siblings. That means that the other fifty percent must come from the parents and the home, right? Wrong! Being brought up in one home versus another accounts, at most, for *five percent* of the differences among people in personality. Identical twins separated at birth are not only similar; they are virtually as similar as identical twins raised together. Adoptive siblings in the same home are not just different; they are about as different as two children plucked from the population at random. The biggest influence that parents have on their children is at the moment of conception.

(I hasten to add that parents are unimportant only when it comes to *differences* among them and differences among their grown children. Anything that *all* normal parents do that affects all children is not measured in these studies. Young children surely need the love, protection, and tutelage of a sane parent. As the psychologist Judith Harris has put it, the studies imply only that children would turn into the same kinds of adults if you left them in their homes and social milieus but switched all the parents around.)

No one knows where the other forty-five percent of the variation comes from. Perhaps personality is shaped by unique events impinging on the growing brain: how the fetus lay in the womb, how much maternal blood it diverted, how it was squeezed during birth, whether it was dropped on its head or caught certain viruses in the early years. Perhaps personality is shaped by unique experiences, like being chased by a dog or receiving an act of kindness from a teacher. Perhaps the traits of parents and the traits of children interact in complicated ways, so that two children growing up with the same parents really have different environments. One kind of parent may reward a rambunctious child and punish a placid one; another kind of parent may do the opposite. There is no good evidence for these scenarios, and I think two others are more plausible, both of which see personality as an adaptation rooted in the divergence of interests between parents and offspring. One is the child's battle plan for competing with its siblings. The other is the child's battle plan for competing in its peer group.

Judith Harris has amassed evidence that children everywhere are socialized by their peer group, not by their parents. At all ages children join various play groups, circles, gangs, packs, cliques, and salons, and they jockey for status within them. Each is a culture that absorbs some customs from the outside and generates many of its own. Children's cultural heritage—the rules of Ringolevio, the melody and lyrics of the nyah-nyah song, the belief that if you kill someone you legally have to pay for his gravestone—is passed from child to child, sometimes for thousands of years. As children grow up they graduate from group to group and eventually join adult groups. Prestige at one level gives one a leg up at the next; most significantly, the leaders of young adolescent cliques are the first to date. At all ages children are driven to figure out what it takes to succeed among their peers and to give these strategies precedence over anything their parents foist on them. Weary parents know they are no match for a child's peers, and rightly obsess over the best neighborhood in which to bring their children up. Many successful people immigrated to this country as children and were not handicapped in the least by culturally inept parents who never learned the language or customs. As a researcher of language development I have always been struck by the way in which children rapidly pick up the language (especially the accent) of their peers, though they spend more time with their parents.

Why aren't children putty in parents' hands? Like Trivers and Harris, I suspect it is because children's genetic interests overlap only partly with their parents'. Children take their calories and protection from their parents, because their parents are the only ones willing to provide them, but they get their information from the best sources they can find and forge their strategies for dealing with life themselves. Their own parents may not be the wisest and most knowledgeable adults around, and worse, the rules at home are often stacked against the children in favor of their born and unborn siblings. And as far as reproduction is concerned, the home is a dead end. The child will have to compete for mates, and before that for the status necessary to find and keep them, in other arenas, which play by different rules. The child had better master them.

Name ______________________ Date ______________ Period ________

Chapter 14

How The Mind Works

1. According to Pinker, what are the five major classifications of personality?

2. In the article, it discusses nature vs. nurture and personality. How much influence does genetics have on the make-up of the personality?

3. What fact about personality development does Pinker believe will shock most people?

Name ______________________ Date ______________ Period ________

Chapter 14

How The Mind Works

4. What two reasons does the author think most likely account for the other 45% of the variation in personality?

5. What does the author mean when he says "As far as reproduction is concerned, the home is a dead end"?

6. Of the five categories listed in the article, at which end of each scale do you think your personality fits?

Chapter 15

Measuring Personality and Personal Abilities

Personality Typing Can Provide Keys to Workplace

Diane Stafford

Ms. Stafford is a free lance writer of psychology and other science-related articles, such as this one about whether people can or should be categorized according to psychological type.

When the lion's away the otters will play. The beavers will keep on working. And the golden retrievers will sit and smile benignly.

That's either a bunch of poppycock or a pretty good picture of the animals in the workplace jungle—if you accept the theory that people can be categorized according to psychological type.

Many educators, psychologists and employment experts believe they can.

Ever since the most widely used personality assessment, the Myers-Briggs Type Indicator, was introduced during World War II, efforts have grown to build teamwork by understanding what makes people tick differently.

Several different personality "tests" are in use. One, which uses animal names to label psychological types, was introduced by counselors Gary Smalley and John Trent. They first applied the lion, otter, beaver and golden retriever appellations to four personalities they defined in their family counseling work.

They and others say personality types can be identified by the way people answer questions about their preferences. By extension, they say, understanding these types can provide keys to workplace, as well as marital, harmony.

"Everyone on our staff knows what they are," said Dennis R. Schemmel, a psychologist and director of the Counseling and Testing Center at the University of Missouri–Kansas City. "And by knowing each other's type, we are more attuned to knowing why each of us reacts the way we do."

UMKC counseling center employees don't use animal names to describe their psychological types. But they can reel off four-letter labels familiar to users of the Myers-Briggs assessment.

Schemmel, for example, is an ISTJ. He describes himself as a logical, detail-oriented person who is well-organized and takes deadlines seriously. He said he is most comfortable thinking through an issue carefully before he draws conclusions or speaks.

The ISTJ label is Myers-Briggs shorthand for one of sixteen personality types obtained by combining four of eight possible preference indicators.

An ISTJ personality, for example, tends to answer Myers-Briggs test questions in such a way as to indicate a preference for:

- Introversion (I) rather than extroversion (E);
- Gathering information by sensing (S) rather than intuition(N);
- Making decisions by thinking (T) rather than feeling (F);
- Preferring to deal with the world with schedules and established judgments (J) rather than spontaneity and looser perceptions (P).

An ISTJ boss, Schemmel said, could clash mightily with an ENFP second in command who is comfortable with improvisation instead of structured plans and with group brainstorming instead of private thoughts. Could clash but won't, if the ISTJ boss understands why the ENFP acts and reacts the way he or she does.

From *Knight-Ridder/Tribune News Service,* Oct 21, 1997 p1021K2496. Reprinted with permission of Knight Ridder/Tribune Information Services.

"You can't change the other guy," Schemmel emphasized. "But understanding this type helps enormously to understand what he's about and to understand there's a way to approach him given his personality."

Psychological type is an explanation of personality developed by the Swiss psychiatrist Carl Jung, who observed that human behavior isn't random. Instead, Jung said, it follows identifiable patterns of inborn preference.

Jungian adherents administer the Myers-Briggs or similar tests to persons aged 14 and older to help discover and define those preferences. A similar test, the Murphy-Meisgeier assessment, is given to children younger than 14.

A year or two ago there was a trend at human resource conferences to include presentations on Enneagrams, a nine-classification personality typing theory. This system labels people as 1s, perfectionists; 2s, givers; 3s, performers; 4s, romantics; 5s, observers; 6s, troopers; 7s, epicures; 8s, bosses; and 9s, mediators, according to their dominant drives.

Another assessment, the Keirsey Temperament Sorter, explained in Please Understand Me by David Keirsey and Marilyn Bates, compacts the four-letter Myers-Briggs types into two-letter labels to identify just four types:

- SJ (sensing/judging);
- SP (sensing/perceiving);
- NF (intuitive/feeling);
- NT (intuitive/thinking).

According to Keirsey, but not yet validated by the extensive follow-up research of the Myers-Briggs test, about 45 percent of people are SJs.

SJs are the types that Smalley calls beavers, the ones most likely to be detailed, deliberate workers, comfortable with following instructions. Smalley said beavers are most likely to react to a new situation by asking, "How was it done in the past?"

Smalley's personality assessment currently is getting wide distribution in Christian churches; his family counseling work is well-known among conservative Christians and those active in Promise Keepers.

Keirsey said about 38 percent of the population are SPs. Smalley calls them the otters. Friendly, fun-loving, verbal and flexible, otters might offer or respond to new proposals with, "Trust me! It'll work out!'

Keirsey's NFs are Smalley's golden retrievers. Keirsey said they represent 10 percent of the population. They are, Smalley posits, loyal, nondemanding and enjoy routine. They are most apt to say, "Let's keep things the way they are."

That would leave about 7 percent as members of Keirsey's NT type. They are Smalley's lions, the goal-driven, action-oriented people who are comfortable taking charge. The lion might say, "Let's do it now!'

Psychological typing is not universally accepted, and even its advocates warn against misuse or too-rigid acceptance of the test results.

All of the assessments are self-selection, which means that people choose the response, generally to a two-choice question, which they believe fits them best.

For example, a Myers-Briggs question asks:

Do you usually
(A) show your feelings freely, or
(B) keep your feelings to yourself?

Depending on the taker's self-perception—and possibly on the answer the taker thinks might be preferred in a certain environment—the self-selections could describe an individual quite different from the one seen by work associates.

Partly because of the capacity to misuse personality indicators, the Kansas City-based Association for Psychological Type exists to educate and promote ethical use and interpretation of psychological type assessments. The association also trains and licenses people to administer the Myers-Briggs assessment.

"It would be misuse, for example, to use Myers-Briggs as a hiring tool," said Julie Sparks, education director at the association. "It should be used only voluntarily and only as a teamwork-building tool.

"We always stress that no questions can fully explain human complexity. No one should ever be pigeonholed because of the indicators."

Association members emphasize that personality typing never should be used as a predictor of competence, capability or job performance.

Typing may be used, though, to indicate tendencies and choices, both of which may influence an individual's happiness in a career path.

Because Myers-Briggs is the granddaddy of personality indicators and has been the subject of the most research, Sparks said she is comfortable advocating only that assessment and the related Murphy-Meisgeier for children.

Any purported test of psychological type, Sparks advises, should be administered "with the understanding that it will reveal inborn preferences, and that is all."

"Never use it as an excuse for behavior," she said, "but do use it as a tool for understanding that someone doesn't behave a certain way just to tick you off.

"If you understand type, you understand it's just normal for them to do that. If you understand type, you understand that we take in information differently, we process it differently and we act on it differently. Understanding type helps you respect those differences and use it to build understanding."

In which case, the otter would understand the lion's need to roar. The beaver would try to cavort with the otter. The lion would dote on the beaver's industry. And the golden retriever probably would just keep being everybody's friend.

❦❦❦

Name ______________________ Date ____________ Period ________

Chapter 15

Personality Typing Can Provide Keys to Workplace

1. Who originally conceived the idea of psychological types?

____

____

____

____

____

____

2. Is psychological typing scientifically proven?

____

____

____

____

____

____

3. What is the benefit of knowing a colleague's personality type?

____

____

____

____

____

____

____

Name ________________ Date ____________ Period ________

Chapter 15

Personality Typing Can Provide Keys to Workplace

4. Why would it be wrong to use the Myers-Briggs personality test as a hiring tool?

5. How would you feel about being given a personality test by your employer? Would you have concerns about being "pigeonholed"?

Coping With Stress

Mihaly Csikszentmihalyi

Mihaly Csikszentmihalyi's theories are also the subject of the Case Study for Chapter 16 in your textbook.

"When a man knows he is to be hanged in a fortnight, it concentrates his mind wonderfully," remarked Samuel Johnson, in a saying whose truth applies to the cases just presented. A major catastrophe that frustrates a central goal of life will either destroy the self, forcing a person to use all his psychic energy to erect a barrier around remaining goals, defending them against further onslaughts of fate; or it will provide a new, more clear, and more urgent goal: to overcome the challenges created by the defeat. If the second road is taken, the tragedy is not necessarily a detriment to the quality of life. Indeed, what objectively seems a devastating event may come to enrich the victims' lives in new and unexpected ways. Even the loss of one of the most basic human faculties, like that of sight, does not mean that a person's consciousness need become impoverished; the opposite is often what happens. But what makes the difference? How does it come about that the same blow will destroy one person, while another will transform it into inner order?

Psychologists usually study the answers to such questions under the heading of *coping with stress.* It is obvious that certain events cause more psychological strain than others: for example, the death of a spouse is several orders of magnitude more stressful than taking out a mortgage on a house, which in turn causes more strain than being given a traffic ticket. But it is also clear that the same stressful event might make one person utterly miserable, while another will bite the bullet and make the best of it. This difference in how a person responds to stressful events has been called "coping ability" or "coping style."

In trying to sort out what accounts for a person's ability to cope with stress, it is useful to distinguish three different kinds of resources. The first is the external support available, and especially the network of social supports. A major illness, for instance, will be mitigated to a certain extent if one has good insurance and a loving family. The second bulwark against stress includes a person's psychological resources, such as intelligence, education, and relevant personality factors. Moving to a new city and having to establish new friendships will be more stressful to an introvert than to an extrovert. And finally, the third type of resource refers to the coping strategies that a person uses to confront the stress.

Of these three factors, the third one is the most relevant to our purposes. External supports by themselves are not that effective in mitigating stress. They tend to help only those who can help themselves. And psychological resources are largely outside our control. It is difficult to become much smarter, or much more outgoing, than one was at birth. But how we cope is both the most important factor in determining what effects stress will have and the most flexible resource, the one most under our personal control.

There are two main ways people respond to stress. The positive response is called a "mature defense" by George Vaillant, a psychiatrist who has studied the lives of successful and relatively unsuccessful Harvard graduates over a period of about thirty years; others call it "transformational coping." The negative response to stress would be a "neurotic defense" or "regressive coping," according to these models.

To illustrate the difference between them, let us take the example of Jim, a fictitious financial analyst who has just been fired from a comfortable job at age forty. Losing one's job is reckoned to be about midpoint in the severity of life stresses; its impact varies, of course, with a person's age and skills, the amount of his savings, and the conditions of the labor market. Confronted with this unpleasant event, Jim can take one of two opposite courses of action. He can withdraw into himself, sleep late, deny what has happened, and avoid thinking about it. He can also discharge his frustration by turning against his family and friends, or disguise it by starting to drink more than usual. All these would be examples of regressive coping, or immature defenses.

Or Jim can keep his cool by suppressing temporarily his feelings of anger and fear, analyzing the problem logically, and reassessing his priorities. Afterward he might redefine what the problem is, so that he can solve it more easily—for instance, by deciding to move to a place where his skills are more in demand, or by retraining himself and acquiring the skills for a new job. If he takes this course, he would be using mature defenses, or transformational coping.

Few people rely on only one or the other strategy exclusively. It is more likely that Jim would get drunk the first night; have a fight with his wife, who had been telling him for years that his job was lousy; and then the following morning, or the week after, he would simmer down and start figuring out what to do next. But people do differ in their abilities to use one or the other strategy. The paraplegic who became a champion archer, or the blind chess master, visited by misfortunes so intense that they are off the scale of stressful life events, are examples of individuals who have mastered transformational coping. Others however, when confronted by much less intense levels of stress, might give up and respond by scaling down the complexity of their lives forever.

The ability to take misfortune and make something good come of it is a very rare gift. Those who possess it are called "survivors," and are said to have "resilience," or "courage." Whatever we call them, it is generally understood that they are exceptional people who have overcome great hardships, and have surmounted obstacles that would daunt most men and women. In fact, when average people are asked to name the individuals they admire the most, and to explain why these men and women are admired, courage and the ability to overcome hardship are the qualities most often mentioned as a reason for admiration. As Francis Bacon remarked, quoting from a speech by the Stoic philosopher Seneca, "The good things which belong to prosperity are to be wished, but the good things that belong to adversity are to be admired."

In one of our studies the list of admired persons included an old lady who, despite her paralysis, was always cheerful and ready to listen to other people's troubles; a teenage camp counselor who, when a swimmer was missing and everybody else panicked, kept his head and organized a successful rescue effort; a female executive who, despite ridicule and sexist pressures, prevailed in a difficult working environment; and Ignaz Semmelweis, the Hungarian physician who in the last century insisted that the lives of many mothers could be saved at childbirth if obstetricians would only wash their hands, even though the rest of the doctors ignored and mocked him. These and many hundreds of others mentioned were respected for the same reasons: They stood firm for what they believed in, and didn't let opposition daunt them. They had courage, or what in earlier time was known simply as "virtue"—a term derived from the Latin word *vir,* or man.

It makes sense, of course, that people should look up to this one quality more than to any other. Of all the virtues we can learn no trait is more useful, more essential for survival, and more likely to improve the quality of life than the ability to transform adversity into an enjoyable challenge. To admire this quality means that we pay attention to those who embody it, and we thereby have a chance to emulate them if the need arises. Therefore admiring courage is in itself a positive adaptive trait; those who do so may be better prepared to ward off the blows of misfortune.

But simply calling the ability to cheat chaos "transformational coping," and people who are good at it "courageous," falls short of explaining this remarkable gift. Like the character in Moliere who said that sleep was caused by "dormitive power," we fail to illuminate matters if we say that effective coping is caused by the virtue of courage. What we need is not only names and descriptions, but an understanding of how the process works. Unfortunately our ignorance in this matter is still very great.

❦❦❦

Name ______________________ Date ______________ Period __________

Chapter 16

Coping With Stress

1. What three different resources determine a person's ability to cope with stress?

2. What are the two main ways people respond to stress?

3. What qualities are associated with transformational coping?

Name ______________________ Date ______________ Period ________

Chapter 16

Coping With Stress

4. "When a man knows he is to be hanged in a fortnight, it concentrates his mind wonderfully." How do these words of Samuel Johnson relate to the article?

5. Can you think of someone you admire for their transformational coping skills?

Melancholy Nation

Joannie M. Schrof and Stacey Schultz

This article looks closely at melancholia and depression and how psychologists are still struggling to understand these conditions.

Mention Prozac to Christine Margaret and she replies with a sardonic laugh. Been there. Zoloft? Tried that. And Paxil. And Elavil and Welbutrin. And a dozen other medications that have failed to alleviate the depression that denies the former actress her sleep, that landed her in the hospital, that left her weighing as little as 80 pounds, and that keeps her from holding a job. "Nobody comprehends what a beast this is," she says. "It has stolen my life."

For more than a decade, Margaret has been suffering privately amid a loud public debate over the merits of the phenomenally famous Prozac and other antidepressants. As 35 million people flocked to Prozac alone, many began to ask: Are too many people taking the drugs, and for the wrong reasons? Do they fundamentally alter personality? Do we as a society expect too much, to be "better than well"?

All but lost in the clamor are some dispiriting facts: Prozac has not turned out to be a magic bullet against depression, and the problem is now worse than ever. In fact, many who study depression say that we are entering an "Age of Melancholy," where people are getting depressed at younger and younger ages, with episodes that are severe and frequent. By some measures, depression has already doubled since World War II, an increase not simply due to greater awareness, says Columbia University epidemiologist Myrna Weissman, but due also to factors such as more stress, fewer family and community ties, even nutritional deficiencies. Depression is on pace to be the world's second-most-disabling disease (after heart disease) by the year 2020; already, the World Health Organization ranks it first among women and fourth overall. In the United States, depression afflicts 18 million people at any given time, 1 in 5 over the course of a lifetime, and costs over $40 billion a year in lost work and health care.

Pills and Pitfalls

To be sure, antidepressant medications and the psychotherapies that often accompany them have been absolute lifesavers for many of the tens of millions of people who have sought help. But 3 out of 10 depression sufferers don't respond at all to a given antidepressant, and the 7 out of 10 who respond do so only partially or find that the benefits wear out. Others cannot tolerate side effects such as gastrointestinal problems, sexual dysfunction, and grogginess. "Given how common depression is, it is a major public health threat that 20 percent of people don't get more than a modest benefit from any of our therapies," says National Institute of Mental Health Director Steven Hyman. This summer, the NIMH will launch an ambitious study to address the problem, which has come to be known as "treatment-resistant depression."

Such studies are desperately needed. Researchers claim that progress has been slowed because many people—including many physicians—still mistake chemical imbalances for weakness of character and don't take the disease seriously. Even though depression takes a greater cumulative toll on society than, say, heart disease, it receives less than one tenth the federal funding. The very name *depression,* some contend, is responsible for much of the problem, because the word is misleading. "People confuse it with the everyday sensation of feeling despondent and dismiss it," says NIMH neuroscientist Philip Gold. "In fact, it takes an incredibly strong person to bear the burden of the disease, which ought to be given a more appropriate name." He suggests "hypothalomo-pituitary-adrenal axis dysfunction"—an appropriately jargony medical description that is accurate but would never make it into the headlines. At least 12 million people are now suffering from the disease without any treatment at all, some with the mistaken belief that one can *will* oneself to be well. For those who do seek help, it's not unusual to consult with as many as three doctors over 10 years just to get the right diagnosis—let alone an effective remedy.

Progress in treating depression has been halting since the disorder was listed in psychiatry's first diagnostic manual in 1952. Early on, it was often treated (like most psychiatric disabilities) with Freudian psychoanalysis, but many experts now consider those techniques counterproductive, largely because exploring the past and focusing on problems exacerbates the tendency to remain "stuck" in negative ruminations. Electroconvulsive therapy—popularly known as electroshock—was and still is one of the most effective treatments against depression, but it requires anesthesia and carries a lingering stigma from a time when ill-trained practitioners caused unnecessary trauma. In the 1970s, researchers turned to two types of medication—so-called tricyclics and monoamine oxidase (MAO) inhibitors—to lessen a great many sufferers' symptoms, but both had serious side effects, and an overdose could cause death.

Mixed Results. It's no wonder then that when Prozac came along in 1988, it was welcomed as a godsend. Even though it is slightly less effective than the earlier antidepressants, its side effects are not as severe. A large number of those who have taken Prozac say they owe their lives to it. But there are problems even for those who do respond. Many who try Prozac and its cousin Zoloft complain of sexual dysfunction or are struck by another bout of depression while still on medication, a problem known as "Prozac poop-out."

That's not to say that current treatments should be abandoned. In fact, some experts are convinced that treatment resistance is as much a failure of the health care system as it is of pharmacology. "I'm convinced that given enough care and expertise, a great many of the people we call treatment resistant could be helped with treatments that are currently available," says Gold. But that is easier said than done at a time when insurers frown on lengthy, time-consuming treatment, he notes. It takes an enormous amount of trial and error to find the right medications and dosages for any given person, and people in the throes of depression are often ill-equipped to persist in the face of treatment failure. Side effects tend to come first, while benefits may not surface for up to six weeks—a period that can seem like an eternity. "Every minute seems like a week when I'm waiting to see if something will work," says Margaret. "My doctor has already tried every medication on the market and thrown up his hands in despair." Yet Bob Olson of Worcester, Mass., is glad he didn't accept the "treatment resistant" label. After 15 medications and 21 ECT sessions, Olson is finally finding relief with Tegretol (a drug that hadn't worked at first) and has been depression free for five years.

These mixed results don't really surprise the experts, given the fact that no one yet knows exactly what depression is. The disorder is so complicated, and manifests itself in so many ways, that most researchers now think of it not as one disease, but many. "I refer to them as the 'depressions,' " says Mark George, a neurologist at the Medical University of South Carolina who uses brain imaging to study depressed patients. "It's obvious from symptoms and from what we see happening in the brain that the people we group together as depressed are suffering from different problems."

For some time, specialists have divided depression into two categories. The first, called "melancholic depression," is marked by hyperarousal in the brain, a sort of chronic stress response that can't turn off and that makes it difficult to sleep or eat. The second, "atypical depression," involves an increase in sleeping and eating, a sort of numb hibernation. Other types, each with different symptoms, continue to emerge, such as seasonal affective disorder, or wintertime depression; dysthymia, a milder but longer-lasting form of depression; cyclothymia, repeating bouts of highs and lows; and the more severe manic depression (or bipolar disorder), which sends sufferers to dangerous, sometimes delusional highs and suicidal lows. "I wouldn't be surprised if, in 10 years, there were 10 known types of depression, each with its own biological abnormalities and each calling for a separate treatment," says George.

As if this weren't complicated enough, it turns out that depression is often entangled with other health problems, making it difficult to tease out one or another problem for treatment. For example, alcoholism often accompanies depression, but antidepressants are not as effective if alcohol (a depressant) is consumed as well. Illnesses as simple as the flu or as serious as heart disease almost always worsen depression, and in turn depression is known to cause a great many physical problems, ranging from bone-density loss to a greater risk of cardiovascular disease and even cancer. In fact, when all other elements are factored out, studies find depressed people at least twice as likely to die during any given period. And that's not counting suicide, an act that a depressed person is 35 times more likely than others to commit.

Spurred by these dire reports, researchers are painstakingly re-examining depressive disorders and developing a far more nuanced understanding of the illnesses. More sophisticated knowledge may not only yield better treatments but also help to erase much of the stigma surrounding depression. Already, the research results are overturning some long-entrenched notions. For instance:

- **Not just sadness.** UCLA neuropsychiatrist Peter Whybrow suggests that people who want to know what severe depression feels like can get a glimpse of it by combining the anguish of profound grief with the bodily sensations of severe jet lag. Boston native and longtime depression sufferer Evie Barkin describes it this way: "It's like the worst migraine of your life, and it seems like it will never go away." Even though depression is called a "mood" disorder, mood is only one of more than a dozen bodily functions interrupted by a depressed, misfiring brain.

  The brain, says Whybrow, has been designed by eons of evolution to strive for harmony with the environment. Depression disrupts that process, so that the brain's basic housekeeping rhythms are thrown off. Sleeping and eating become disordered (along with libido), and energy levels dissipate, so that the simplest chore or social interaction can seem impossible. Further, the depressed brain fires off counterproductive distress signals of doom, gloom, fear, anxiety, panic, and self-destruction. Cognitive abilities like concentration and memory are sabotaged. In fact, the symptoms are so varied that it can be hard to recognize that a person has depression. One person may eat constantly and be unable to sit still, while the next may seem like a zombie. Another may suffer severe headaches, muscle pain, and upset stomach.
- **The myth of misfortune.** Depression is not caused by bad circumstances or cured by good ones, even though it often seems that way to a sufferer. It's a cruel trick of the brain that when everything feels wrong, it's almost impossible for a victim to recognize brain malfunction as the source of the problem. As a result, the depressed person looks for an explanation in the events of the world. Certainly, stressful events—the death of a loved one, for example—can trigger depression, but only in someone whose brain is vulnerable to the disease, which Whybrow labels a "neurobiological Achilles heel." That's why the disease runs in families, and also why, although most people experience grief when a loved one dies, only 5 percent develop clinical depression.

Paradoxically, the real-world triggers for depression and the illness itself frequently decouple once the disorder is set in motion. When a severe brain disorder takes over, it causes suffering that is "only distantly related" to sad life events, according to Whybrow, and that does not ease when circumstances improve. The upside to this is that even those people who would seem to have every reason to stay depressed can often be helped. For example, University of Iowa neuropsychiatrist Robert Robinson finds that most stroke victims who become depressed quickly respond to treatment. "Even though they are unable to talk, walk, or feed themselves," says Robinson, "they are mentally well and ready to make the most of what they are left with."

While good or bad circumstances cannot dictate the course of depression, the way people think about them can exert either a damaging or a palliative effect. Typically, the depressed brain's misguided stress signals foster rumination and worry, which in turn fuel further detrimental physiological reactions and worsen the disease. It *is* possible to learn to avoid thoughts that exacerbate the brain's already-out-of-whack stress response, but such mind control is difficult enough for a healthy individual, let alone one whose brain is caught in red-alert mode.

That's why psychotherapy can be so critical in treating the illness. Most psychiatrists now believe that in severe depression, medication is needed to restore enough bodily and cognitive functioning for a sufferer to then attack the unhealthy thinking that has grown out of the illness. Most of the more than 20 types of psychotherapy show some success with depression, but those with the best track record are designed to be fairly short, lasting less than a year, and focus on correcting distorted thought patterns. For example, a typical way of thinking that exacerbates depression is known as the "romantic worldview," in which a person crumbles whenever circumstances don't turn out as planned. Working with a therapist, depression sufferers learn to adopt more of a "tragic" worldview (the philosophical belief that for every loss something is gained, and vice versa), which tends to reduce stress-inducing thoughts.

The most therapeutic thing about counseling may ultimately be the genuine concern a therapist shows for a patient. "Depression turns people on themselves, and they enter therapy expecting a therapist to see them as negatively as they see themselves," says NIMH's Gold. "When that doesn't happen, a trust develops that allows a patient to re-examine faulty assumptions."

• **Not a happy pill.** Many people shy away from medication, and others are suspicious of those who take it, because of a misguided notion that antidepressants alter the personality, providing a fast, false high. "People always tell me they don't want to alter themselves," says Gold. "But I tell them they already are altered, and the medication will restore them to their normal state." Antidepressants work slowly, as the brain responds to the medication by restructuring its faulty messaging machinery. In normal brains, the antidepressants do not elevate mood.

• **A lifelong disorder.** It can be especially devastating when, after a year of medication and therapy—just about when life seems to be getting back to normal—a person is clobbered by another depression for no apparent reason. Until recently, recurrences of depression were thought to be a rare exception to the rule, but now scientists know otherwise. The majority of sufferers first experience depression by adolescence, and it tends to surface in regular cycles, lasting an average of nine to 16 months and then remitting for a similar period. Given this cycling, says Richard Glass, deputy editor of the *Journal of the American Medical Association,* it is best to manage it like any other chronic illness, such as diabetes or high blood pressure. While many people now take antidepressants until they feel better, Glass and others recommend that they continue for at least 18 months after the depression lifts. Still other clinicians feel that, given the enormous consequences of relapse, it is not unwise to keep severe depression sufferers on medication for life.

• **The serotonin craze.** Prozac acts on the brain chemical serotonin, and in part because of the drug's initial hype, that one neurotransmitter has been singled out as the prime culprit behind depression. But depression cannot be explained by a shortage of any single brain substance. "Nothing disturbs me more than when someone tries to describe something as complicated as a mental state with something as simplistic as serotonin levels," says Hyman. "It's as if the brain were nothing but a water bottle full of chemicals." Although often branded the brain's "feel good" chemical, serotonin is just one of several substances the brain uses to regulate its sense of well-being. Dopamine, for example, is a chemical that seems to drive the brain's reward systems, and some of the older antidepressants act upon it. It is also the chemical implicated in addictions and could explain why depression and substance abuse go hand in hand. Similarly, the neurotransmitter norepinephrine appears to act as the brain's watchdog, firing when there is cause for worry or fear. Norepinephrine is probably a key player in the neurological underpinnings of depression's anxious features. Melatonin, a chemical that governs sleep cycles, seems to be off kilter in winter depression.

Hormones that bathe the brain also play a role in depression. Much of the worst long-term damage from depression can be linked to cortisol, a stress hormone. It is harmless in small doses but ravages the body when pumped continuously into the system by depression or anxiety. The sex hormones also seem to be involved in depression and may explain why the disorder is so common in adolescence—and also why women (who have more variable levels of sex hormones) appear more vulnerable to depression than do men.

In addition to biochemical changes, brain structures themselves appear to behave differently in depression. In imaging studies, the left prefrontal cortex seems to be especially sluggish. And studies of depression sufferers who have improved, both after medication and after therapy, show an increase in that region's activity. One study even shows that the left prefrontal cortex is more active following exercise, offering a physiological explanation for why workouts elevate mood. In addition to the prefrontal cortex, connected centers deep in the primitive, emotional brain are also implicated in depression. In one study of people hit with depression for the first time after age 65, brain scans showed that 85 percent of them had actually suffered a "silent" or unknown stroke in one of these regions. Silent strokes in other areas of the brain do not cause depression.

New Treatments

Armed with a better understanding of depression, researchers are developing new ways to conquer it. At least 18 new antidepressants are in the pharmaceutical pipeline, and most of them attempt to attack depression through just one or two of the chemical pathways. (Unfortunately, each time a brain chemical is tinkered with, a host of side effects appears, making it infeasible to design a medication that would alter several chemicals at once.) Pharmacia & Upjohn, for example, is working on an antidepressant that targets norepinephrine. Other companies are looking at drugs to inhibit a chemical known as corticotropin-releasing factor, the substance that tells the pituitary and adrenal glands to flood the body with cortisol. And some are studying a chemical known as Substance P. Still others are developing new drug-delivery systems, such as skin patches, which may alleviate many side effects by releasing the medication very slowly.

Jump-Start

Scientists have long searched for a depression treatment that works faster, and now they think they've found it. Using a promising experimental procedure known as "rapid transcranial magnetic stimulation," scientists say they are getting results after six days. A new twist on an old idea, RTMS uses a powerful magnet to deliver an electric jolt to the brain, in the same fashion as electroconvulsive therapy but without electric stimulation to unnecessary parts of the brain. The idea is something like a defibrillator for the heart: The electric voltage that passes through the brain causes many neurons to fire at once, and something about this action seems to reset the rate at which the brain releases the various chemicals implicated in depression.

In clinical trials of RTMS, many of those patients who have failed to respond to several other treatments improve within a week, and the vast majority are significantly better after two weeks of 20-minute RTMS sessions. No one yet knows whether the beneficial effects of RTMS last for longer than six months, but that is likely to be determined by the time RTMS is approved for general use in another two to three years. "It could be a great thing to use in conjunction with medication," says George of the Medical University of South Carolina. "RTMS could step in first to offer fast relief, then medication could kick in later to maintain well-being over the long haul."

The science of depression has advanced to the point where even the most cautious researchers speak of finding a true cure in their lifetime. "I'm very optimistic about our ability to lick this disease medically," says former NIMH director Frederick Goodwin. But he is more pessimistic about social elements—stresses that fuel depression and misguided notions that keep it shrouded in shame. "I still have people tell me that I should cheer up because I have nothing to be depressed about," Margaret says. "As if I had a choice in the matter."

Name ______________________ Date ______________ Period ________

Chapter 17

Melancholy Nation

1. How many kinds of depression are there?

2. Why is psychotherapy often helpful in treating depression?

3. Do anti-depressant pills alter personality?

Name ______________________ Date ______________ Period __________

Chapter 17

Melancholy Nation

4. What are some of the major stumbling blocks to the successful diagnosis of depression?

5. What are your personal feelings about anti-depressants? Would you be willing to take them if you were suffering from *mild* depression?

"I Never Thought It Would Happen to Me"

Irvin D. Yalom

Dr. Irvin Yalom is the author of a highly regarded 1980 textbook, Existential Psychotherapy. *His bestselling work* Love's Executioner *shows how such neuroses as eating disorders can be alleviated by bringing patients' death-anxieties to the surface. He is a Standford Medical School professor.*

I greeted Elva in my waiting room, and together we walked the short distance to my office. Something had happened. She was different today, her gait labored, discouraged, dispirited. For the last few weeks there had been a bounce in her steps, but today she once again resembled the forlorn, plodding woman I had first met eight months ago. I remember her first words then: "I think I need help. Life doesn't seem worth living. My husband's been dead for a year now, but things aren't getting any better. Maybe I'm a slow learner."

But she hadn't proved to be a slow learner. In fact, therapy had progressed remarkably well—maybe it had been going too easily. What could have set her back like this?

Sitting down, Elva signed and said, "I never thought it would happen to me."

She had been robbed. From her description it seemed an ordinary purse snatching. The thief, no doubt, spotted her in a Monterey seaside restaurant and saw her pay the check in cash for three friends—elderly widows all. He must have followed her into the parking lot and, his footsteps muffled by the roaring of the waves, sprinted up and, without breaking stride, ripped her purse away and leaped into his nearby car.

Elva, despite her swollen legs, hustled back into the restaurant to call for help, but of course it was too late. A few hours later, the police found her empty purse dangling on a roadside bush.

Three hundred dollars meant a lot to her, and for a few days Elva was preoccupied by the money she had lost. That concern gradually evaporated and in its place was left a bitter residue—a residue expressed by the phrase "I never thought it would happen to me." Along with her purse and her three hundred dollars, an illusion was snatched away from Elva—the illusion of personal specialness. She had always lived in the privileged circle, outside the unpleasantness, the nasty inconveniences visited on ordinary people—those swarming masses of the tabloids and newscasts who are forever being robbed or maimed.

The robbery changed everything. Gone was the coziness, the softness in her life; gone was the safety. Her home had always beckoned her with its cushions, gardens, comforters, and deep carpets. Now she saw locks, doors, burglar alarms, and telephones. She had always walked her dog every morning at six. The morning stillness now seemed menacing. She and her dog stopped and listened for danger.

None of this is remarkable. Elva had been traumatized and now suffered from commonplace post-traumatic stress. After an accident or an assault, most people tend to feel unsafe, to have a reduced startle threshold, and to be hypervigilant. Eventually time erodes the memory of the event, and victims gradually return to their prior, trusting state.

But for Elva it was more than a simple assault. Her world view was fractured. She had often claimed, "As long as a person has eyes, ears, and a mouth, I can cultivate their friendship." But no longer. She had lost her belief in benevolence, in her personal invulnerability. She felt stripped, ordinary, unprotected. The true impact of that robbery was to shatter illusion and to confirm, in brutal fashion, her husband's death.

Of course, she knew that Albert was dead. Dead and in his grave for over a year and a half. She had taken the ritualized widow walk—through the cancer diagnosis; the awful, retching, temporizing chemotherapy; their last visit together to Carmel; their last drive down El Camino Real; the hospital bed at home; the funeral; the paperwork; the ever-dwindling dinner invitations; the widow and widower's clubs; the long, lonely nights. The whole necrotic catastrophe.

Yet, despite all this, Elva had retained her feeling of Albert's continued existence and thereby of her persisting safety and specialness. She had continued to live "as if," as if the world were safe, as if Albert were there, back in the workshop next to the garage.

Mind you, I do not speak of delusion. Rationally, Elva knew Albert was gone, but still she lived her routine, everyday life behind a veil of illusion which numbed the pain and softened the glare of the knowing. Over forty years ago, she had made a contract with life whose explicit genesis and terms had been eroded by time but whose basic nature was clear: Albert would take care of Elva forever. Upon this unconscious premise, Elva had built her entire assumptive world—a world featuring safety and benevolent paternalism.

Albert was a fixer. He had been a roofer, an auto mechanic, a general handyman, a contractor; he could fix anything. Attracted by a newspaper or magazine photograph of a piece of furniture or some gadget, he would proceed to replicate it in his workshop. I, who have always been hopelessly inept in a workshop, listened in fascination. Forty-one years of living with a fixer is powerfully comforting. It was not hard to understand why Elva clung to the feeling that Albert was still there, out back in the workshop looking out for her, fixing things. How could she give it up? Why should she? That memory, reinforced by forty-one years of experience, had spun a cocoon around Elva that shielded her from reality—that is, until her purse was snatched.

Upon first meeting Elva eight months before, I could find little to love in her. She was a stubby, unattractive woman, part gnome, part sprite, part toad, and each of those parts ill tempered. I was transfixed by her facial plasticity: she winked, grimaced, and popped her eyes either singly or in duet. Her brow seemed alive with great washboard furrows. Her tongue, always visible, changed radically in size as it darted in and out or circled her moist, rubbery, pulsating lips. I remember amusing myself, almost laughing aloud, by imagining introducing her to patients on long-term tranquilizer medication who had developed tardive dyskinesia (a drug-induced abnormality of facial musculature). The patients would, within seconds, become deeply offended because they would believe Elva to be mocking them.

But what I really disliked about Elva was her anger. She dripped with rage and, in our first few hours together, had something vicious to say about everyone she knew—save, of course, Albert. She hated the friends who no longer invited her. She hated those who did not put her at ease. Inclusion or exclusion, it was all the same to her: she found something to hate in everyone. She hated the doctors who had told her that Albert was doomed. She hated even more those who offered false hope.

Those hours were hard for me. I had spent too many hours in my youth silently hating my mother's vicious tongue. I remember the games of imagination I played as a child trying to invent the existence of someone she did not hate: A kindly aunt? A grandfather who told her stories? An older playmate who defended her? But I never found anyone. Save, of course, my father, and he was really part of her, her mouthpiece, her animus, her creation who (according to Asimov's first law of robotics) could not turn against his maker—despite my prayers that he would once—just once, please, Dad—pop her.

All I could do with Elva was to hold on, hear her out, somehow endure the hour, and use all my ingenuity to find something supportive to say—usually some vapid comment about how hard it must be for her to carry around that much anger. At times I, almost mischievously, inquired about others of her family circle. Surely there must be someone who warranted respect. But no one was spared. Her son? She said his elevator "didn't go to the top floor." He was "absent": even when he was there, he was "absent." And her daughter-in-law? In Elva's words, "a GAP"—gentile American princess. When driving home, her son would call his wife on his automobile telephone to say he wanted dinner right away. No problem. She could do it. Nine minutes, Elva reminded me, was all the time required for the GAP to cook dinner—to "nuke" a slim gourmet TV dinner in the microwave.

Everyone had a nickname. Her granddaughter, "Sleeping Beauty" (she whispered with an enormous wink and a nod), had two bathrooms—two, mind you. Her housekeeper, whom she had hired to attenuate her loneliness, was "Looney Tunes," and so dumb that she tried to hide her smoking by exhaling the smoke down the flushing toilet. Her pretentious bridge partner was "Dame May Whitey" (and Dame May Whitey was spry-minded compared with the rest, with all the Alzheimer zombies and burned-out drunks who, according to Elva, constituted the bridge-playing population of San Francisco).

But somehow, despite her rancor and my dislike of her and the evocation of my mother, we got through these sessions. I endured my irritation, got a little closer, resolved my countertransference by disentangling my mother from Elva, and slowly, very slowly, began to warm to her.

I think the turning point came one day when she plopped herself in my chair with a "Whew! I'm tired." In response to my raised eyebrows, she explained she had just played eighteen holes of golf with her twenty-year-old nephew. (Elva was sixty, four foot eleven, and at least one hundred sixty pounds.)

"How'd you do?" I inquired cheerily, keeping up my side of the conversation.

Elva bent forward, holding her hand to her mouth as though to exclude someone in the room, showed me a remarkable number of enormous teeth, and said "I whomped the shit out of him!"

It struck me as wonderfully funny and I started to laugh, and laughed until my eyes filled with tears. Elva liked my laughing. She told me later it was the first spontaneous act from Herr Doctor Professor (so that was *my* nickname!), and she laughed with me. After that we got along famously. I began to appreciate Elva—her marvelous sense of humor, her intelligence, her drollness. She had led a rich, eventful life. We were similar in many ways. Like me, she had made the big generational jump. My parents arrived in the United States in their twenties, penniless immigrants from Russia. Her parents had been poor Irish immigrants, and she had straddled the gap between the Irish tenements of South Boston and the duplicate bridge tournaments of Nob Hill in San Francisco.

At the beginning of therapy, an hour with Elva meant hard work. I trudged when I went to fetch her from the waiting room. But after a couple of months, all that changed. I looked forward to our time together. None of our hours passed without a good laugh. My secretary said she always could tell by my smile that I had seen Elva that day.

We met weekly for several months, and therapy proceeded well, as it usually does when therapist and patient enjoy each other. We talked about her widowhood, her changed social role, her fear of being alone, her sadness at never being physically touched. But, above all, we talked about her anger—about how it had driven away her family and her friends. Gradually she let it go; she grew softer and more gentle. Her tales of Looney Tunes, Sleeping Beauty, Dame May Whitey, and the Alzheimer bridge brigade grew less bitter. Rapprochements occurred; as her anger receded, family and friends reappeared in her life. She had been doing so well that, just before the time of the purse snatching, I had been considering raising the question of termination.

But when she was robbed, she felt as though she were starting all over again. Most of all, the robbery illuminated her ordinariness, her "I never thought it would happen to me" reflecting the loss of belief in her personal specialness. Of course, she was still special in that she had special qualities and gifts, that she had a unique life history, that no one who had ever lived was just like her. That's the rational side of specialness. But we (some more than others) also have an irrational sense of specialness. It is one of our chief methods of denying death, and the part of our mind whose task it is to mollify death terror generates the irrational belief that we are invulnerable—that unpleasant things like aging and death may be the lot of others but not our lot, that we exist beyond law, beyond human and biological destiny.

Although Elva responded to the purse snatching in ways that *seemed* irrational (for example, proclaiming that she wasn't fit to live on earth, being afraid to leave her house), it was clear that she was *really* suffering from the stripping away of irrationality. That sense of specialness, of being charmed, of being the exception, of being eternally protected—all those self-deceptions that had served her so well suddenly lost their persuasiveness. She saw through her own illusions, and what illusion had shielded now lay before her, bare and terrible.

Her grief wound was now fully exposed. This was the time, I thought, to open it wide, to debride it, and to allow it to heal straight and true.

"When you say you never thought it would happen to you, I know just what you mean," I said. "It's so hard for me, too, to accept that all these afflictions—aging, loss, death—are going to happen to me, too."

Elva nodded, her tightened brow showing that she was surprised at my saying anything personal about myself.

"You must feel that if Albert were alive, this would never have happened to you." I ignored her flip response that if Albert were alive she wouldn't have been taking those three old hens to lunch. "So the robbery brings home the fact that he's really gone."

Her eyes filled with tears, but I felt I had the right, the mandate, to continue "You knew that before, I know. But part of you didn't. Now you really know that he's dead. He's not in the yard. He's not out back in the workshop. He's not anywhere. Except in your memories."

Elva was really crying now, and her stubby frame heaved with sobs for several minutes. She had never done that before with me. I sat there and wondered, "*Now* what do I do?" But my instincts luckily led me to what proved to be an inspired gambit. My eyes lit upon her purse—that same ripped-off, much abused purse; and I said, "Bad luck is one thing, but aren't you asking for it carrying around something that large?" Elva, plucky as ever, did not fail to call attention to my overstuffed pockets and the clutter on the table next to my chair. She pronounced the purse "medium-sized."

"Any larger," I responded, "and you'd need a luggage carrier to move it around."

"Besides," she said, ignoring my jibe, "I need everything in it."

"You've got to be joking! Let's see!"

Getting into the spirit of it, Elva hoisted her purse onto my table, opened its jaws wide, and began to empty it. The first items fetched forth were three empty doggie bags.

"Need two extra ones in case of an emergency?" I asked.

Elva chuckled and continued to disembowel the purse. Together we inspected and discussed each item. Elva conceded that three packets of Kleenex and twelve pens (plus three pencil stubs) were indeed superfluous, but held firm about two bottles of cologne and three hairbrushes, and dismissed, with an imperious flick of her hand, my challenge to her large flashlight, bulky notepads, and huge sheaf of photographs.

We quarreled over everything. The roll of fifty dimes. Three bags of candies (low-calorie, of course). She giggled at my question: "Do you believe, Elva, that the more of these you eat, the thinner you will become?" A plastic sack of old orange peels ("You never know, Elva, when these will come in handy"). A bunch of knitting needles ("Six needles in search of a sweater," I thought). A bag of sourdough starter. Half of a paperback Steven King novel (Elva threw away sections of pages as she read them: "They weren't worth keeping," she explained). A small stapler ("Elva, this is crazy!"). Three pairs of sunglasses. And, tucked away into the innermost corners, assorted coins, paper clips, nail clippers, pieces of emery board, and some substance that looked suspiciously like lint.

When the great bag had finally yielded all, Elva and I stared in wonderment at the contents set out in rows on my table. We were sorry the bag was empty and that the emptying was over. She turned and smiled, and we looked tenderly at each other. It was an extraordinarily intimate moment. In a way no patient had ever done before, she showed me everything. And I had accepted everything and asked for even more. I followed her into her every nook and crevice, awed that one old woman's purse could serve as a vehicle for both isolation and intimacy: the absolute isolation that is integral to existence and the intimacy that dispels the dread, if not the fact, of isolation.

That was a transforming hour. Our time of intimacy—call it love, call it love making—was redemptive. In that one hour, Elva moved from a position of forsakenness to one of trust. She came alive and was persuaded, once more, of her capacity for intimacy.

I think it was the best hour of therapy I ever gave.

❦❦❦

Name ______________________ Date ______________ Period ________

Chapter 18

"I Never Thought It Would Happen to Me"

1. What was Elva's immediate reaction to the robbery of her purse?

2. In the beginning of her therapy, what was the author's relationship with Elva?

3. What qualities did the author eventually come to appreciate in Elva?

Name ______________________ Date ______________ Period ________

Chapter 18

"I Never Thought It Would Happen to Me"

4. What event does Yalom believe Elva equated the robbery?

5. Do you think it is important for people to think of themselves as special, or do you think it is deluding yourself? Write a paragraph on how you think of yourself as truly special.

Chapter 19 Sociocultural Influences and Relationships

The American Way of Blame

Martin E. P. Seligman

Dr. Seligman is a prominent and distinguished psychologist who is active in many organizations. His concern here is with understanding and preventing outbreaks of violence in our schools.

In the last year there has been a cascade of multiple murders in school by American boys. In the 1950s there were none. What changed, and do these changes give us some clues about how to end this nightmare?

The outer world of boys has, of course, changed, but their inner world has changed as well—in an astonishing and dismaying way. The outer changes are better known, but they bear repeating: easy access to guns, contagion fostered by the media and the waning of parental supervision.

The psychological changes are even more frightening. Traditional American child-rearing in individual responsibility has been replaced by a self-esteem movement. This movement tells parents and educators that their first duty is to make kids feel good about themselves. Kids are taught mantras like "I am special," and they believe them. Low self-esteem is seen as the cause of teen-age pregnancy, depression, suicide, drug abuse and violence, and so teaching self-esteem is supposed to be a vaccine.

A Recipe for Violence

Unfortunately it turns out that hit men, genocidal maniacs, gang leaders and violent kids often have high self-esteem, not low self-esteem. A recipe for their violence is a mean streak combined with an unwarranted sense of self-worth. When such a boy comes across a girl or parents or schoolmates who communicate to him that he is not all that worthy, he lashes out.

To top it off, our kids are imbued with victimology, which today has become the American way of blame. It is too routine for adults and their kids to explain all their problems as victimization. When a boy in trouble sees himself as a victim, this festers into seething anger. With easy availability of guns, it can explode as murder.

The tabloid reporting of mass murder feeds into this state of the child's mind and so is contagious. Murder is reported on the front page and leads the nightly news in gory color and audible sobbing. The airing of the shattered emotions of the victims' families and friends is only marginally newsworthy, yet it goes on for days, and has a galvanizing effect on the potential copycat.

All this occurs against a background of kids watching several hours of TV daily with about one murder per hour. When killing becomes routine entertainment, the inhibitions against killing melt. For the child who feels victimized by other kids and his parents and his schoolteachers, being able to fantasize so concretely about wreaking this vengeance is empowering and delicious. These outer and inner changes suggest a short-term stop gap and long-term solution. Every secondary school should consider installing metal detectors right away. When a weapon is found on any student, the right move is not just to expel, but to talk. A psychologist may be able to see the difference between a schoolyard bully and a potential killer.

What's Required to Stop It

In the long run, we need much more than metal detectors. There are more competent experts than I am to spell out how to limit access to guns, how to change the reporting of mass murder and how to persuade parents to spend more time with their kids. What I believe needs changing is the way kids think about their troubles. Baseless self-esteem is easily shattered by the usual setbacks of growing up; when, in a boy with a mean streak, it combines with blaming parents, peers and the schools—blaming anyone but himself—it can become violent. We need to teach our children warranted self-esteem and realistic optimism—based on the skills of doing well in the world, on doing well with others and on personal responsibility. These research-based programs improve the ways that all kids think about their troubles, manage emotions, solve problems and communicate with others. But when it comes to aggression, counseling—which focuses only on the child—has limits. Programs involving the family and the school do much better. Whole communities suffer the consequences of schoolyard violence, and whole communities are required to stop it.

❦❦❦

Name ________________________ Date ______________ Period ________

Chapter 19

The American Way of Blame

1. What are some of the "outer ways" that life has changed for American teenage boys?

2. What are some of the "inner ways" that life has changed for American teenage boys?

3. According to Seligman, what has been the effect of the self-esteem movement on society?

Name ______________________ Date ______________ Period ________

Chapter 19

The American Way of Blame

4. What is victimology?

5. What other factors does Seligman cite as contributing to violence in teens?

6. Do you agree with Seligman's assessment of this situation? Why or why not? Would you add other factors as more important?

Chapter 20 Sociocultural Influences: Attitudes and Beliefs

Where Bias Begins: The Truth About Stereotypes

Annie Murphy Paul

This article first appeared in the May/June 1998 issue of Psychology Today. *It focuses on how everyone, everyday, uses stereotypes and makes biased decisions.*

Psychologists Once Believed That Only Bigoted People Used Stereotypes. Now the Study of Unconscious Bias Is Revealing the Unsettling Truth: We All Use Stereotypes, All the Time, Without Knowing It. We Have Met the Enemy of Equality, and the Enemy Is Us.

Mahzarin Banaji doesn't fit anybody's idea of a racist. A psychology professor at Yale University, she studies stereotypes for a living. And as a woman and a member of a minority ethnic group, she has felt firsthand the sting of discrimination. Yet when she took one of her own tests of unconscious bias, "I showed very strong prejudices," she says. "It was truly a disconcerting experience." And an illuminating one. When Banaji was in graduate school in the early 1980s, theories about stereotypes were concerned only with their explicit expression: outright and unabashed racism, sexism, anti-Semitism. But in the years since, a new approach to stereotypes has shattered that simple notion. The bias Banaji and her colleagues are studying is something far more subtle, and more insidious: what's known as automatic or implicit stereotyping, which, they find, we do all the time without knowing it. Though out-and-out bigotry may be on the decline, says Banaji, "if anything, stereotyping is a bigger problem than we ever imagined."

Previously, researchers who studied stereotyping and simply asked people to record their feelings about minority groups and had used their answers as an index of their attitudes. Psychologists now understand that these conscious replies are only half the story. How progressive a person seems to be on the surface bears little or no relation to how prejudiced he or she is on an unconscious level—so that a bleeding-heart liberal might harbor just as many biases as a neo-Nazi skinhead. As surprising as these findings are, they confirmed the hunches of many students of human behavior. "Twenty years ago, we hypothesized that there were people who said they were not prejudiced but who really did have unconscious negative stereotypes and beliefs," says psychologist Jack Dovidio, Ph.D., of Colgate University. "It was like theorizing about the existence of a virus, and then one day seeing it under a microscope."

The test that exposed Banaji's hidden biases—and that this writer took as well, with equally dismaying results—is typical of the ones used by automatic stereotype researchers. It presents the subject with a series of positive or negative adjectives, each paired with a characteristically "white" or "black" name. As the name and word appear together on a computer screen, the person taking the test presses a key, indicating whether the word is good or bad. Meanwhile, the computer records the speed of each response.

A glance at subjects' response times reveals a startling phenomenon: Most people who participate in the experiment—even some African-Americans—respond more quickly when a positive word is paired with a white name or a negative word with a black name. Because our minds are more accustomed to making these associations, says Banaji, they process them more rapidly. Though the words and names aren't subliminal, they are presented so quickly that a subject's ability to make deliberate choices is diminished—allowing his or her underlying assumptions to show through. The same technique can be used to measure stereotypes about many different social groups, such as homosexuals, women, and the elderly.

The Unconscious Comes Into Focus

From these tiny differences in reaction speed—a matter of a few hundred milliseconds—the study of automatic stereotyping was born. Its immediate ancestor was the cognitive revolution of the 1970s, an explosion of psychological research into the way people think. After decades dominated by the study of observable behavior, scientists wanted a closer look at the more mysterious operation of the human brain. And the development of computers—which enabled scientists to display information very quickly and to measure minute discrepancies in reaction time—permitted a peek into the unconscious.

At the same time, the study of cognition was also illuminating the nature of stereotypes themselves. Research done after World War II—mostly by European emigres struggling to understand how the Holocaust had happened—concluded that stereotypes were used only by a particular type of person: rigid, repressed, authoritarian. Borrowing from the psychoanalytic perspective then in vogue, these theorists suggested that biased behavior emerged out of internal conflicts caused by inadequate parenting.

The cognitive approach refused to let the rest of us off the hook. It made the simple but profound point that we all use categories—of people, places, things—to make sense of the world around us. "Our ability to categorize and evaluate is an important part of human intelligence," says Banaji. "Without it, we couldn't survive." But stereotypes, are too much of a good thing. In the course of stereotyping, a useful category—say, women—becomes freighted with additional associations, usually negative. "Stereotypes are categories that have gone too far," says John Bargh, Ph.D., of New York University. "When we use stereotypes, we take in the gender, the age, the color of the skin of the person before us, and our minds respond with messages that say hostile, stupid, slow, weak. Those qualities aren't out there in the environment. They don't reflect reality." Bargh thinks that stereotypes may emerge from what social psychologists call in-group/out-group dynamics. Humans, like other species, need to feel that they are part of a group, and as villages, clans, and other traditional groupings have broken down, our identities have attached themselves to more ambiguous classifications, such as race and class. We want to feel good about the group we belong to—and one way of doing so is to denigrate all those who aren't in it. And while we tend to see members of our own group as individuals, we view those in out-groups as an undifferentiated—stereotyped—mass. The categories we use have changed, but it seems that stereotyping itself is bred in the bone.

Though a small minority of scientists argues that stereotypes are usually accurate and can be relied upon without reservations, most disagree—and vehemently. "Even if there is a kernel of truth in the stereotype, you're still applying a generalization about a group to an individual, which is always incorrect," says Bargh. Accuracy aside, some believe that the use of stereotypes is simply unjust. "In a democratic society, people should be judged as individuals and not as members of a group," Banaji argues. "Stereotyping flies in the face of that ideal."

Predisposed to Prejudice

The problem, as Banaji's own research shows, is that people can't seem to help it. A recent experiment provides a good illustration. Banaji and her colleague, Anthony Greenwald, Ph.D., showed people a list of names—some famous, some not. The next day, the subjects returned to the lab and were shown a second list, which mixed names from the first list with new ones. Asked to identify which were famous, they picked out the Margaret Meads and the Miles Davises—but they also chose some of the names on the first list, which retained a lingering familiarity that they mistook for fame. (Psychologists call this the "famous overnight-effect.") By a margin of two-to-one, these suddenly "famous" people were male.

Participants weren't aware that they were preferring male names to female names, Banaji stresses. They were simply drawing on an unconscious stereotype of men as more important and influential than women. Something similar happened when she showed subjects a list of people who might be criminals: without knowing they were doing so, participants picked out an overwhelming number of African-American names. Banaji calls this kind of stereotyping IMPLICIT, because people know they are making a judgment—but just aren't aware of the basis upon which they are making it.

Even further below awareness is something that psychologists call automatic processing, in which stereotypes are triggered by the slightest interaction or encounter. An experiment conducted by Bargh required a group of white participants to perform a tedious computer task. While performing the task, some of the participants were subliminally exposed to pictures of African-Americans with neutral expressions. When the subjects were then asked to do the task over again, the ones who had been exposed to the faces reacted with more hostility to the request—because, Bargh believes, they were responding in kind to the hostility which is part of the African-American stereotype. Bargh calls this the "immediate hostile reaction," which he believes can have a real effect on race relations. When African-Americans accurately perceive the hostile expressions that their white counterparts are unaware of, they may respond with hostility of their own—thereby perpetuating the stereotype.

Of course, we aren't completely under the sway of our unconscious. Scientists think that the automatic activation of a stereotype is immediately followed by a conscious check on unacceptable thoughts—at least in people who think that they are not prejudiced. This internal censor successfully restrains overtly biased responses. But there's still the danger of leakage, which often shows up in non-verbal behavior: our expressions, our stances, how far away we stand, how much eye contact we make.

The gap between what we say and what we do can lead African-Americans and whites to come away with very different impressions of the same encounter, says Jack Dovidio. "If I'm a white person talking to an African-American, I'm probably monitoring my conscious beliefs very carefully and making sure everything I say agrees with all the positive things I want to express," he says. "And I usually believe I'm pretty successful because I hear the right words coming out of my mouth." The listener who is paying attention to non-verbal behavior, however, may be getting quite the opposite message. An African-American student of Dovidio's recently told him that when she was growing up, her mother had taught her to observe how white people moved to gauge their true feelings toward blacks. "Her mother was a very astute amateur psychologist—and about 20 years ahead of me," he remarks.

Where Does Bias Begin?

So where exactly do these stealth stereotypes come from? Though automatic-stereotype researchers often refer to the unconscious, they don't mean the Freudian notion of a seething mass of thoughts and desires, only some of which are deemed presentable enough to be admitted to the conscious mind. In fact, the cognitive model holds that information flows in exactly the opposite direction: connections made often enough in the conscious mind eventually become unconscious. Says Bargh: "If conscious choice and decision making are not needed, they go away. Ideas recede from consciousness into the unconscious over time."

Much of what enters our consciousness, of course, comes from the culture around us. And like the culture, it seems that our minds are split on the subjects of race, gender, class, sexual orientation. "We not only mirror the ambivalence we see in society, but also mirror it in precisely the same way," says Dovidio. Our society talks out loud about justice, equality, and egalitarianism, and most Americans accept these values as their own. At the same time, such equality exists only as an ideal, and that fact is not lost on our unconscious. Images of women as sex objects, footage of African-American criminals on the six o'clock news,—"this is knowledge we cannot escape," explains Banaji. "We didn't choose to know it, but it still affects our behavior."

We learn the subtext of our culture's messages early. By five years of age, says Margo Monteith, Ph.D., many children have definite and entrenched stereotypes about blacks, women, and other social groups. Adds Monteith, professor of psychology at the University of Kentucky: "Children don't have a choice about accepting or rejecting these conceptions, since they're acquired well before they have the cognitive abilities or experiences to form their own beliefs." And no matter how progressive the parents, they must compete with all the forces that would promote and perpetuate these stereotypes: peer pressure, mass media, the actual balance of power in society. In fact, prejudice may be as much a result as a cause of this imbalance. We create stereotypes—African-Americans are lazy, women are emotional—to explain why things are the way they are. As Dovidio notes, "Stereotypes don't have to be true to serve a purpose."

Why Can't We All Get Along?

The idea of unconscious bias does clear up some nettlesome contradictions. "It accounts for a lot of people's ambivalence toward others who are different, a lot of their inconsistencies in behavior," says Dovidio. "It helps explain how good people can do bad things." But it also prompts some uncomfortable realizations. Because our conscious and unconscious beliefs may be very different—and because behavior often follows the lead of the latter—"good intentions aren't enough," as John Bargh puts it. In fact, he believes that they count for very little. "I don't think free will exists," he says, bluntly—because what feels like the exercise of free will may be only the application of unconscious assumptions.

Not only may we be unable to control our biased responses, we may not even be aware that we have them. "We have to rely on our memories and our awareness of what we're doing to have a connection to reality," says Bargh. "But when it comes to automatic processing, those cues can be deceptive." Likewise, we can't always be sure how biased others are. "We all have this belief that the important thing about prejudice is the external expression of it." says Banaji. "That's going to be hard to give up."

One thing is certain: We can't claim that we've eradicated prejudice just because its outright expression has waned. What's more, the strategies that were so effective in reducing that sort of bias won't work on unconscious beliefs. "What this research is saying is that we are going to have to change dramatically the way we think we can influence people's behaviors," says Banaji. "It would be naive to think that exhortation is enough." Exhortation, education, political protest—all of these hammer away at our conscious beliefs while leaving the bedrock below untouched. Banaji notes, however, that one traditional remedy for discrimination—affirmative action—may still be effective since it bypasses our unconsciously compromised judgment.

But some stereotype researchers think that the solution to automatic stereotyping lies in the process itself. Through practice, they say, people can weaken the mental links that connect minorities to negative stereotypes and strengthen the ones that connect them to positive conscious beliefs. Margo Monteith explains how it might work. "Suppose you're at a party and someone tells a racist joke—and you laugh," she says. "Then you realize that you shouldn't have laughed at the joke. You feel guilty and become focused on your thought processes. Also, all sorts of cues become associated with laughing at the racist joke: the person who told the joke, the act of telling jokes, being at a party, drinking." The next time you encounter these cues, "a warning signal of sorts should go off—'wait, didn't you mess up in this situation before?'—and your responses will be slowed and executed with greater restraint."

That slight pause in the processing of a stereotype gives conscious, unprejudiced beliefs a chance to take over. With time, the tendency to prevent automatic stereotyping may itself become automatic. Monteith's research suggests that, given enough motivation, people may be able to teach themselves to inhibit prejudice so well that even their tests of implicit bias come clean.

The success of this process of "de-automatization" comes with a few caveats, however. First, even its proponents concede that it works only for people disturbed by the discrepancy between their conscious and unconscious beliefs, since unapologetic racists or sexists have no motivation to change. Second, some studies have shown that attempts to suppress stereotypes may actually cause them to return later, stronger than ever. And finally, the results that Monteith and other researchers have achieved in the laboratory may not stick in the real world, where people must struggle to maintain their commitment to equality under less-than-ideal conditions. Challenging though that task might be, it is not as daunting as the alternative researchers suggest: changing society itself. Bargh, who likens de-automatization to closing the barn door once the horses have escaped, says that "it's clear that the way to get rid of stereotypes is by the roots, by where they come from in the first place." The study of culture may someday tell us where the seeds of prejudice originated; for now, the study of the unconscious shows us just how deeply they're planted.

Name ______________________ Date ______________ Period __________

Chapter 20

Where Bias Begins: The Truth About Stereotypes

1. Automatic stereotyping records how fast a person reacts to a stimulus. Why is how fast a person reacts to a word-stimulus an indictor of unconscious bias?

2. What is the difference between categorizing and stereotyping?

3. Why does the author claim that stereotyping is undemocratic?

Name ______________________ Date ______________ Period ________

Chapter 20

Where Bias Begins: The Truth About Stereotypes

4. Why are some psychologists studying automatic stereotyping interested in body language?

5. Assuming you accept the reality of automatic stereotyping, what do you think are the most effective ways to mitigate (reduce) its effects?

Answer Key

Answers for Chapter 1—
The Field of Psychology
Who Is the Cat That Curiosity Killed?
by Elizabeth Loftus

1. This idea is the basis of the author's argument. She argues that perception is often inaccurate, and that evidence is the only sound basis for forming an opinion.
2. No. The purpose of the author's second question, "What exactly is the evidence?", is to determine the reliability of the facts being presented as evidence.
3. The story of the curiosity cat is significant because it is a frequently-quoted piece of wisdom which becomes meaningless once it is analyzed.
4. Answers will vary. However, the article mentions that eyewitness testimony, an important form of evidence which is based on memory, is frequently unreliable.
5. Answer will vary.

Answers for Chapter 2—
Methods of Psychology
Folk Wisdom: Was Your Grandmother Right?
by Robert Epstein, Ph.D.

1. He defines folk wisdom as a kind of unreliable, inconsistent kind of wisdom that all cultures pass along.
2. Epstein wanted to know if folk (or psychology) wisdom could hold up to scientific examination when looked at using methods employed by social scientists.
3. James Pennebaker concluded that for about 66% of people, self-disclosure (or confession) is psychologically beneficial. It is not beneficial when it is forced, or when the audience is likely to be judgmental.
4. The author insists that discipline is absolutely necessary for effective parenting, but it must be applied with affection and emotional support.
5. Answers will vary.

Answers for Chapter 3—
Brain, Body, and Behavior
The Brain Has a Mind of Its Own
by Richard Restak

1. The limbic system governs aggressive behavior.
2. Emotions and feelings work independently of rational thought and can be illogical.
3. A person's behavior is influenced by his/her environment; behaviors and personality traits can be genetically determined; an individual's behavior is influenced by genes, environment, and the surrounding society.
4. Answers will vary.
5. Answers will vary.

Answers for Chapter 4—
Sensation and Perception
Phantoms in the Brain
by V. S. Ramachandran and Sandra Blakeslee

1. Thurber saw wild and vivid images that he did not imagine—they came "unbidden."
2. Charles Bonnet syndrome is a condition that causes extreme visual "hallucinations" in people with damage to their visual pathway—in the eye or in the brain.
3. Many people who "see" the vivid images are afraid other people will think they are hallucinating. They are afraid their families will think they are "losing their mind."
4. Both involve feeling or seeing something that is not really "there." People who experience Charles Bonnet syndrome and people who feel phantom limbs claim that it is just like reality—even more intense.

Answers for Chapter 5—
Motivation and Emotion
The Educated Heart by Daniel Goleman

1. The ability to emphasize with others and to control impulses, to recognize feelings, and to interact harmoniously.
2. No.
3. If deficiencies can be predicted they may be prevented.
4. Effective emotional literacy programs are taught over many years. They repeat basic lessons throughout the grades, emphasize the school as a community, and inculcate a core set of values, such as self-awareness, self-control, empathy, and cooperation.
5. Answers will vary. Students can feel intimated when they feel they are being pressured into sharing their feelings, or when they feel their behavior is being criticized. This is especially likely when emotional literacy classes are used as a kind of correctional or remedial course.

Answers for Chapter 6—Consciousness
Sleep Thieves: An Eye-opening Exploration into the Science and Mysteries of Sleep by Stanley Coren

1. The author claims that while children (age 6–12) sleep an average of 10 hours per night, by the time a person reaches the age of 12 he or she is getting by on less than 6 and 1/2 hours of sleep. By age 18, that figure has dropped to 6 or fewer hours. He believes many adolescents are running up a sleep debt.
2. While many adults catch up on sleep during the weekend, most adolescents actually sleep few hours over the weekend. This exacerbates the effect of the sleep debt.
3. Symptoms include a reduction in alertness and performance levels in talks that require focused attention, precise movements, memory, problem solving and other cognitive skills. It is harder to awaken someone suffering from general lack of sleep.
4. Content requiring rote memorization may be retained in short term memory long enough to pass a test. For those exams that require problem solving and creative thinking, it is more important get facts into long term memory and to get enough sleep to be able to use logic and organizational skills on the information.
5. Answers will vary.

Answers for Chapter 7—
Principles of Learning
On Responsibility and Punishment by John Staddon

1. A psychological theory which holds that a person's behavior is determined by his genetic heritage and his environment.
2. Punishment is ineffective; punishment provokes counterattack; positive reinforcement is more effective than punishment.
3. Deterrence.
4. Determinism allows us to predict the effect of punishment. If punishment had no predictable effect, it would be pointless to use it.
5. Answers will vary.

Answers for Chapter 8—
Information Processing and Memory
It's Magical! It's Malleable! It's . . . Memory by Jill Neimark

1. Elizabeth Loftus is a research psychologist specializing in repressed memories. This article is about the reliability of these memories.
2. Repressed memories have been used as the basis for lawsuits and criminal prosecutions. Changes have been made to statutes depending upon whether or not these memories can be relied upon.
3. It is the ability of the memory to repeat experiences with some flexibility (making mistakes) that allows for adaptation to the environment. Repetition is not the same as remembrance.
4. The hippocampus (sea-horse shaped) is critical for learning (and thus forming memories). It processes, discards, and dispatches information by sending signals to other parts of the brain.

5. Scientists suspect that two powerful stress hormones released in the dangerous fight or flight situation (adrenaline and noradenaline) have a powerful effect upon the neurons involved in memory storage.
6. Memory will often get the general core content of a situation or time correct without being as accurate in the peripheral details. The mind cannot reconstruct exactly what happens as well as it can reproduce the general tone.
7. Answers will vary.

Answers for Chapter 9—
Intelligence and Creativity
How To Make a Better Student: Seven Kinds of Smart by James Collins

1. The author wants the reader to decide whether the increasing practice of schools to teaching methodologies on the seven multiple intelligences is good education.
2. Their main criticism is that there is no solid evidence or proof of Gardner's claims. Gardner claims that developing a test to measure intelligence is counterintuitive.
3. The author makes the point that the school systems do not really understand or properly apply Gardner's concepts. He also explains that different children respond to different teaching methods—not that all children should be taught with all intelligences.
4. Many people believe that a lack of success in the traditional academic environment should not be an indication that the child is not intelligent. Parents would rather think that the tests are not asking the right questions in the right way.
5. It would be very difficult to structure a business or educational work environment that does emphasize language, math, and communication skills and the most important.
6. Answers will vary.

Answers for Chapter 10—
Infancy and Childhood
Jean Piaget by Seymour Papert

1. The discovery was that children's thought processes were logical and orderly for their stage of development; that the thought processes of children were not the same as the processes adults used.
2. Piaget's work has come to have a deep influence on the work of educational reformers to follow in the footsteps of Dewey, Montessori, and Friere. His theories examined the way children learned.
3. Piaget was afraid that constant correction was teaching children not to hypothesize and make them afraid to develop original explanations for events.
4. Epistemology is the theory of knowledge; it is the science that examines how we know things.
5. Answers will vary.

Answers for Chapter 11—Adolescence
Adolescent Friends Not Always a Bad Influence by Hugh McIntosh

1. The three findings are (1) crowds (cliques) help ease the transition from childhood to adulthood; (2) teens usually encourage each other in positive rather than negative ways; and (3) parents may have more influence than they realize.
2. Teens are in a development state where conformity is very important. It is easier to conform with similarly minded people than very different people.
3. Unlike positive peer groups, members of deviant groups don't usually have a knowledge or psychological maturity to give constructive advice or support.
4. Authoritative parenting allows for the maximum control while still allowing some negotiating on individual, day-to-day issues. Good management skills were also an effective way to influence adolescents.
5. Answers will vary.

Answers for Chapter 12—
Adulthood and Aging
Brain Power by Joannie M. Schrof

1. Answers can include: Brain power always declines with old age; old age causes memory loss; exercising your mind will protect it from mental decay; illness increases the likelihood of mental deterioration in old age; old brains are incapable of rejuvenation or adaptation.
2. Rigid adherence to routine; low satisfaction with life; negative emotions, such as depression, anxiety and anger.
3. Moderate exercise seems to increase brain power. Excessive exercise can decrease cognitive ability.
4. Characteristics associated with wisdom include: Sound judgment, perspective, ability to weigh conflicting values and generate problem-solving strategies. Wisdom is based on experience and empathy, while intelligence is related to IQ.
5. Answer will vary but may include: positive attitude; higher level of education; a complex and stimulating lifestyle; a smart spouse; regular exercise; emotional well-being.

Answers for Chapter 13—Gender Differences
Gender Stereotypes and Roles by Susan Basow

1. Taboo against displays of anger; competition for males.
2. For women, intimacy typically involves sharing feelings and concerns. For men, it typically involves activities and impersonal discussions.
3. Competitiveness; need to suppress feelings.
4. Answers will vary. The article mentions that women's social conditioning assists them in forming nurturing relationships. Otherwise, it clearly emphasizes that conventional gender roles have a negative impact on both same-sex and cross-sex friendships.
5. Answers will vary.

Answers for Chapter 14—
Theories of Personality
How the Mind Works by Steven Pinker

1. The five major classifications of personality are extroversion/introversion; neuroticism/stability; agreeableness/antagonism; conscientiousness/undirectedness; and openness/nonopenness.
2. According to Pinker, approximately 50% of the personality is the result of genetic make-up.
3. Pinker believes that most people would be shocked to know that parents and the environment account for only about 5% of the differences among people raised together.
4. Two reasons suggested by the author include the child's way of competing with his/her siblings and competition within the peer group.
5. Answers will vary, but should address the theory that competition for mates will depend on skills learned from the peer group, not the parents.
6. Answers will vary but should address the theory that skills needed for finding a mate are developed from competition with the peer group and not the parents.

Answers for Chapter 15—
Measuring Personality and Personal Abilities
Personality Typing Can Provide Keys to Workplace by Diane Stafford

1. Carl Jung.
2. No.
3. It could help you to understand why a colleague reacts a certain way, and how (s)he is likely to process information. It could also help you become attuned to each other's differences.
4. The Myers-Briggs test is not intended to be a predictor of competence, capability or job performance. It does not measure intelligence; it only indicates mental and emotional tendencies.
5. Answers will vary.

Answers for Chapter 16—
Conflict, Stress, and Coping
Flow, The Psychology of Optimal Experience
by Mihaly Csikszentmihalyi

1. External support, such as family and friends; psychological resources, such as intelligence and education; coping strategies.
2. Transformational coping and regressive coping.
3. Courage, resilience, virtue, persistence, faith, etc.
4. Johnson implies that a major catastrophe will alter a person's perspective, offering an ironic opportunity for growth.
5. Answers will vary.

Answers for Chapter 17—Mental Disorders
Melancholy Nation
by Joannie Schrof and Stacey Schultz

1. The main categories of depression are melancholic and atypical depression. However, doctors are continuously uncovering new kinds of depression.
2. Psychotherapy can help patients learn to avoid stress-inducing thoughts. The trust and feelings of concern that develop between the patient and therapist are also beneficial.
3. No. Anti-depressants are intended to correct existing chemical imbalances caused by depression.
4. Many people, including physicians, do not take depression seriously; many sufferers refuse to seek medical help; the symptoms of depression vary widely, which makes it difficult to diagnose.
5. Answers will vary.

Answers for Chapter 18—
Treatment and Therapy
"I Never Thought It Would Happen to Me"
from* Love's Executioner *by Irvin Yalom

1. Elva suffered from post-traumatic stress. Her feeling of specialness and security had been destroyed. Her "world-view" was fractured.
2. The therapist was not fond of her. He associated her meanness, anger, and sharp tongue with his own mother's unpleasant personality.
3. He discovered a sense of humor and wit that he appreciated and created a strong bond between them.
4. Yalom believed that Elva interpreted the robbery as a loss of her specialness, in the sense that she was not going to age and die as others. The robber made her feel her mortality.
5. Answers will vary.

Answers for Chapter 19—
Sociocultural Influences and Relationships
The American Way of Blame
by Martin Seligman

1. Some of the outer ways include easy access to guns, contagion fostered by the media, and the waning of parental supervision.
2. According to the author, self-esteem movements have become more important than effective parenting measures.
3. The effect has been to teach children that it is more important to feel good than to "behave good." It has too often developed an inflated sense of self-worth.
4. Victimology is the practice of blaming other people and situations rather than examining the actions of the individual for responsibility.
5. Other factors include the amount of violence in the entertainment industry and the need to deal constructively (using psychologists) with youth who have been identified as being prone to using violence.
6. Answers will vary.

Answers for Chapter 20—
Sociocultural Influences: Attitudes and Beliefs
Where Bias Begins: The Truth About Stereotypes by Annie Murphy Paul

1. A fast reaction is an indication that the brain has made this kind of association before, that the neurons are travelling "familiar" routes.
2. Categorizing is a necessary skill that helps us navigate through daily life. In stereotyping, unnecessary emotional (and usually negative) associations are added to the categories.
3. Stereotyping is applying generalizations to a group rather than at individuals.
4. Body language can reveal unconscious attitudes toward people. When perceived by a member of the stereotyped group, this can create hostility that is turned back on the individual.
5. Answers will vary but should address becoming more familiar with members of other groups and making a conscious effort to analyze your reactions when prejudice or bias occurs.

